THE
TENDER
WARR†OR

The Life of David · Volume 1

DAVID JEREMIAH

with Dr. David Jeremiah

Contents

ABOUT
DR. DAVID JEREMIAH
AND TURNING POINT

Dr. David Jeremiah is the founder of Turning Point, a ministry committed to providing Christians with sound Bible teaching relevant to today's changing times through radio and television broadcasts, audio series, books, and live events. Dr. Jeremiah's common-sense teaching on topics such as family, prayer, worship, angels, and biblical prophecy forms the foundation of Turning Point.

David and his wife, Donna, reside in El Cajon, California, where he serves as the senior pastor of Shadow Mountain Community Church. David and Donna have four children and twelve grandchildren.

In 1982, Dr. Jeremiah brought the same solid teaching to San Diego television that he shares weekly with his congregation. Shortly thereafter, Turning Point expanded its ministry to radio. Dr. Jeremiah's inspiring messages can now be heard worldwide on radio, television, and the Internet.

Because Dr. Jeremiah desires to know his listening audience, he travels nationwide holding ministry rallies that touch the hearts and lives of many people. According to Dr. Jeremiah, "At some point in time, everyone reaches a turning point; and for every person, that moment is unique, an experience to hold onto forever. There's so much changing in today's world that sometimes it's difficult to choose the right path. Turning Point offers people an understanding of God's Word as well as the opportunity to make a difference in their lives."

Dr. Jeremiah has authored numerous books, including *Escape the Coming Night* (Revelation), *The Handwriting on the Wall* (Daniel), *Overcoming Loneliness*, *God in You* (Holy Spirit), *When Your World Falls Apart*, *My Heart's Desire*, *31 Days to Happiness—Searching for Heaven on Earth*, *Captured by Grace*, *What in the World Is Going On?*, *The Coming Economic Armageddon*, *I Never Thought I'd See the Day!*, *What Are You Afraid Of?*, *Agents of the Apocalypse*, *RESET—Ten Steps to Spiritual Renewal*, *Ten Questions Christians Are Asking*, and *People Are Asking . . . Is This the End?*

How to Use This Study Guide

T he purpose of this Turning Point study guide is to reinforce
Dr. David Jeremiah's dynamic, in-depth teaching and to aid the
reader in applying biblical truth to his or her daily life. This
study guide is designed to be used in conjunction with Dr. Jeremiah's
The Tender Warrior – Volume 1 audio series, but it may also be used
by itself for personal or group study.

Structure of the Lessons

Each lesson is based on one of the messages in the *The Tender
Warrior – Volume 1* compact disc series and focuses on specific passages
in the Bible. Each lesson is composed of the following elements:

- *Outline*

The outline at the beginning of the lesson gives a clear, concise
picture of the topic being studied and provides a helpful framework
for readers as they listen to Dr. Jeremiah's teaching.

- *Overview*

The overview summarizes Dr. Jeremiah's teaching on the
passage being studied in the lesson. Readers should refer to the
Scripture passages in their own Bibles as they study the overview.
Unless otherwise indicated, Scripture verses quoted are taken from
the New King James Version.

- *Personal and Group Application Questions*

This section contains a variety of questions designed to help
readers dig deeper into the lesson and the Scriptures, and to apply
the lesson to their daily lives. For Bible study groups or Sunday
school classes, these questions will provide a springboard for group
discussion and interaction.

- *Did You Know?*

This section presents a fascinating fact, historical note, or insight
that adds a point of interest to the preceding lesson.

Personal Study

Thank you for selecting *The Tender Warrior – Volume 1* for your current study. The lessons in this study guide were created to help you gain fresh insights into God's Word and develop new perspectives on topics you may have previously studied. Each lesson is designed to challenge your thinking, and help you grow in your knowledge of Christ. During your study, it is our prayer that you will discover how biblical truth affects every aspect of your life and your relationship with Christ will be strengthened.

When you commit to completing this study guide, try to set apart a time, daily or weekly, to read through the lessons without distraction. Have your Bible nearby when you read the study guide, so you're ready to look up verses if you need to. If you want to use a notebook to write down your thoughts, be sure to have that handy as well. Take your time to think through and answer the questions. If you plan on reading the study guide with a small group, be sure to read ahead and be prepared to take part in the weekly discussions.

Leader's Guide

Thank you for your commitment to lead a group through *The Tender Warrior*. Being a leader has its own rewards. You may discover that your walk with the Lord deepens through this experience. Throughout the study guide, your group will explore new topics and review study questions that encourage thought-provoking group discussion.

The lessons in this study guide are suitable for Sunday school classes, small-group studies, elective Bible studies, or home Bible study groups. Each lesson is structured to provoke thought and help you grow in your knowledge and understanding of God. There are multiple components in this section that can help you structure your lessons and discussion time, so make sure you read and consider each one.

Before You Begin

Before you begin each meeting, make sure you and your group are well-versed with the content of the chapter. Every person should have his or her own study guide so they can follow along and write in the study guide if need be. When possible, the study guide should be used with the corresponding compact disc series. You may wish to assign the study guide lesson as homework prior to the meeting of the group and then use the meeting time to listen to the CD and discuss the lesson.

To ensure that everyone has a chance to participate in the discussion, the ideal size for a group is around eight to ten people. If there are more than ten people, try to break up the bigger group into smaller subgroups. Make sure the members are committed to participating each week, as this will help create stability and help you better prepare the structure of the meeting.

At the beginning of the study each week, start the session with a question to challenge group members to think about the issues you will be discussing. The members can answer briefly, but the goal is to have an idea in their mind as you go over the lesson. This allows the group members to become engaged and ready to interact with the group.

After reviewing the lesson, try to initiate a free-flowing discussion. Invite group members to bring questions and insights they may have discovered to the next meeting, especially if they were unsure of the meaning of some parts of the lesson. Be prepared to discuss how biblical truth applies to the world we live in today.

Weekly Preparation

As the group leader, here are a few things you can do to prepare for each meeting:

- Choose whether or not you will play the CD message during your small group session.

  If you decide to play the CD message from Dr. Jeremiah as part of the meeting, you will need to adjust the group time accordingly.

- Make sure you are thoroughly familiar with the material in the lesson.

  Make sure you understand the content of the lesson so you know how to structure group time and you are prepared to lead group discussion.

- Decide, ahead of time, which questions you plan to discuss.

  Depending on how much time you have each week, you may not be able to reflect on every question. Select specific questions which you feel will evoke the best discussion.

- Take prayer requests.

  At the end of your discussion, take prayer requests from your group members and pray for each other.

Structuring the Discussion Time

If you need help in organizing your time when planning your group Bible study, here are two schedules, for sixty minutes and ninety minutes, which can give you a structure for the lesson:

Option 1 (Listen to Audio CD)	60 Minutes	90 Minutes
Welcome: Members arrive and get settled.	N/A	5 minutes
Getting Started Question: Prepares the group for interacting with one another.	Welcome and Getting Started 5 minutes	15 minutes
Message: Listen to the audio CD.	40 minutes	40 minutes
Discussion: Discuss group study questions.	10 minutes	25 minutes
Prayer and Application: Final application for the week and prayer before dismissal.	5 minutes	5 minutes

Option 2 (No Audio CD)	60 Minutes	90 Minutes
Welcome: Members arrive and get settled.	5 minutes	10 minutes
Getting Started Question: Prepares the group for interacting with one another.	10 minutes	10 minutes
Message: Review the lesson.	15 minutes	25 minutes
Discussion: Discuss group study questions.	25 minutes	35 minutes
Prayer and Application: Final application for the week and prayer before dismissal.	5 minutes	10 minutes

As the group leader, it is up to you to keep track of the time and keep things moving along according to your schedule. If your group is having a good discussion, don't feel the need to stop and move on to the next question. Remember, the purpose is to pull together ideas, and share unique insights on the lesson. Make time each week to discuss how to apply these truths to living for Christ today.

The purpose of discussion is for everyone to participate, but don't be concerned if certain group members are more quiet—they may be internally reflecting on the questions and need time to process their ideas before they can share them.

Group Dynamics

Leading a group study can be a rewarding experience for you and your group members—but that doesn't mean there won't be challenges. Certain members may feel uncomfortable discussing topics that they consider very personal, and might be afraid of being called on. Some members might have disagreements on specific issues. To help prevent these scenarios, consider the following ground rules:

- If someone has a question that may seem off topic, suggest that it is discussed at another time, or ask the group if they are okay with addressing that topic.

- If someone asks a question you don't know the answer to, confess that you don't know and move on. If you feel comfortable, invite other group members to give their opinions, or share their comments based on personal experience.

- If you feel like a couple of people are talking much more than others, direct questions to people who may not have shared yet. You could even ask the more dominating members to help draw out the quiet ones.

- When there is a disagreement, encourage the group members to process the matter in love. Invite members from opposing sides to evaluate their opinions and consider the ideas of the other members. Lead the group through Scripture that addresses the topic, and look for common ground.

When issues arise, remind your group to think of Scripture: "Love one another" (John 13:34), "If it is possible, as much as depends on you, live peaceably with all men" (Romans 12:18), and "Be quick to listen, slow to speak and slow to become angry" (James 1:19, NIV).

FOR CONTINUING STUDY

For a complete listing of Dr. Jeremiah's materials for personal and group study call 1-800-947-1993, go online to www.DavidJeremiah.org, or write to Turning Point, P.O. Box 3838, San Diego, CA 92163.

Dr. Jeremiah's *Turning Point* program is currently heard or viewed around the world on radio, television, and the Internet in English. *Momento Decisivo*, the Spanish translation of Dr. Jeremiah's messages, can be heard on radio in every Spanish speaking country in the world. The television broadcast is also broadcast by satellite throughout the Middle East with Arabic subtitles.

Contact Turning Point for radio and television program times and stations in your area, or visit our website at www.DavidJeremiah.org/stationlocator.

THE TENDER WARRIOR
THE LIFE OF DAVID
VOLUME 1

INTRODUCTION

On the night of June 17, 1972, a security guard at the Watergate office complex in Washington, D.C., made a seemingly insignificant discovery: a piece of tape on a basement door leading to the parking garage. When the police arrived, they found five burglars in the offices of the Democratic National Committee.

Thus began one of the darkest periods in the history of American politics, a period that concluded with the resignation of the sitting president, Richard M. Nixon—the only American president in history ever to resign the office.

It took more than two years for the drama to run its course, but on August 9, 1974, President Nixon submitted his letter of resignation. The "smoking gun" was a tape recording made in the Oval Office of the White House just a few days after the Watergate break-in. President Nixon had steadfastly refused to release this tape, and for good reason—it implicated the president and one of his aides in an attempt to cover up the investigation of the Watergate burglary and other activities. He resigned just days after the Supreme Court ruled that the tape had to be released.

The nation was stunned. It is said that 85 percent of Americans who owned television sets were tuned to the Senate hearings concerning the Watergate affair. People could not believe that a president who was enjoying popularity in the post-Vietnam era would have stooped so low as to become involved in such a tawdry affair as the Watergate burglaries and attempted cover-up.

It has been said that the best of men are capable of the worst, and the worst of men are capable of the best. Nowhere is that made more plain than in the stories of the sweet singer of Israel, David: the son of Jesse, the man after God's own heart. David was a young man who won the heart of his nation as a teenager when he stepped onto the stage of history as a man of courage and faith. After being anointed to replace the disobedient King Saul, David saved Saul from the disgrace of defeat by the Philistine army when he single-handedly killed the Philistine giant, Goliath.

With Saul's kingship having been terminated by God, it seemed an orderly transition would soon take place. Instead, both Saul and David began respective downward spirals into sin that threw the nation into turmoil and resulted in death for Saul and shame and humiliation for David.

When Saul became king, he stood head and shoulders above his contemporaries and appeared to be the king who would establish Israel's prominence among her neighbors. But he violated his kingly prerogatives twice by disobedience, became insanely jealous of David and tried to murder him, ordered the murder of more than fifty priests and an entire village of people who had helped David, pursued David relentlessly around Judea, and ultimately consulted a medium when God stopped responding to him.

David fared little better: He became a liar and a deceiver, a pillager responsible for the destruction of numerous towns on the borders of Israel, and became the bodyguard of the king of Israel's archenemy, the Philistines.

In this study guide, you will follow the intertwined stories of these two good men gone bad—and you'll discover why God took Saul's life but preserved David's. And therein lies the secret to David's ultimate greatness: He was a tender warrior who had a heart for God. David's failures provide some of the most dramatic lessons learned in all of Scripture, and his own heartbreaking revelations in the psalms he penned show the depth of the pain resulting from his choices.

This first volume in *The Tender Warrior* series will introduce you to a man who ultimately learned firsthand about the tender mercies of his God.

INTRODUCTION TO DAVID

1 Samuel 8–15

In this lesson we are introduced to David,
a man after God's own heart.

OUTLINE

Some people seem to have it all: good looks, great talent, and a contagious personality. Sometimes it is hard to relate to such people until we learn they have weaknesses like everyone else. We realize that if God can use them in spite of their failures, He can use us as well.

I. **David Was Great Because of His Context**
   A. The Context of His Life Historically
   B. The Context of His Life Personally
   C. The Context of His Life Biblically

II. **David Was Great Because of His Charisma**
   A. David Was a Man of Physical Charisma
   B. David Was a Man of Personal Charisma
   C. David Was a Man of National Charisma

III. **David Was Great Because of His Creativity**

IV. **David Was Great Because of the Choice of His Life**

V. **David Was Great Because of the Confession of His Life**

To the best of my knowledge, there is no person in biblical or secular recorded history with the name David prior to the Bible's David. Even after we meet David in the Old Testament, no other biblical figure has that name. Today, however, many thousands of people bear that name or know someone named David. It is a testament not only to the uniqueness of the name but to history's fascination with this famous character in biblical history.

In Hebrew, David means "beloved," and the David we will meet in this series of lessons has certainly become dearly loved by many—and for many good reasons.

DAVID WAS GREAT BECAUSE OF HIS CONTEXT

There are three kinds of context that must be understood in order to capture a complete picture of who David was: historical, personal, and biblical.

The Context of His Life Historically

Some people are born at a time in life for which their gifts seem particularly suited: George Washington, Abraham Lincoln, and Dr. Martin Luther King, Jr. come to mind. David was also present at a time when Israel needed him. The five centuries prior to David had witnessed the nation of Israel declining in every way. After Israel's last great leader, Joshua, things began going downhill. Enemies of Israel tormented the nation during the period of the judges, and God always raised up a deliverer. Samuel was the last of these deliverers, or judges, from whom the people in Israel demanded a king (1 Samuel 8:5).

As a result, God gave Samuel permission to anoint Saul to be the king over Israel. Instead of God ruling over them, the people wanted an earthly king like the surrounding nations. First Samuel 9 describes Saul, a striking man who stood head and shoulders over his peers. Gifted, tall, and handsome, Saul seemed to be a good choice for king; but his reign was short, ending in disgrace. Saul angered the Lord by taking upon himself the role of priest, offering a sacrifice he shouldn't have, and by disobeying the Lord in his dealings with the Amalekites (1 Samuel 15). Saul's disobedience was the last straw, and God rejected him as king.

God then instructed Samuel to go to Bethlehem to the house of Jesse where he would find a successor to Saul. That successor was David, the youngest of Jesse's sons, whom Saul found tending his father's sheep. Historically, Israel was in dire need of someone to sit upon the throne who would lead the nation in righteousness. And David became that man.

The Context of His Life Personally

David appears to have come from a humble family setting—there is no evidence of servants in the household. (David himself was out tending the sheep when Samuel arrived.) And within the family, David appears to have been so young and seemingly insignificant that Jesse did not even have him stand with the rest of his sons before Samuel. Samuel did not see the next king among Jesse's other sons and had to ask if there were others. Almost as an afterthought, Jesse remembered David, who was in the fields with the sheep. David had a tender attitude toward his parents, at one point secreting them from Bethlehem to be protected by the king of Moab when Saul was seeking to kill him.

On another occasion, when he was hiding from Saul, David longed for a drink of water from the well at Bethlehem, his home. Three of his men broke through the Philistine lines and brought back water from Bethlehem for their commander. David was so touched that he refused to drink it, pouring it out as an offering to the Lord (2 Samuel 23:15–16). David loved his family and his home.

The Context of His Life Biblically

David is mentioned in the New Testament more than any other Old Testament figure—a total of 56 times in the Gospels, Acts, Epistles, and Revelation. Only fourteen chapters of the Bible are given over to the life of Abraham, but 62 chapters are devoted to the story of David. He occupies as commanding a presence in the Old Testament as the Son of David does in the New Testament.

DAVID WAS GREAT BECAUSE OF HIS CHARISMA

David exhibited three different kinds of charisma: physical, personal, and national.

David Was a Man of Physical Charisma

David was charismatic in the true sense of the word, not the modern religious sense. He apparently was not tall (Eliab, his brother, seems to have been taller—1 Samuel 16:6), and he couldn't fit in Saul's armor (1 Samuel 17:39). But he was athletic, quick, and strong as revealed in his various exploits. He was also handsome—"glowing with health and had a fine appearance and handsome features" (1 Samuel 16:12, NIV). David was also talented, being skilled as a harp player (1 Samuel 16:18). When he was first described to Saul, the description included his ability to play the harp, bravery as a warrior, eloquence, and handsome appearance (verse 18). He must have been quite a charmer based on the Bible's description!

David Was a Man of Personal Charisma

David was a multitalented and multifaceted person, gifted in many different ways. A musician, a warrior, an exile, a leader, a king, a good friend, a humble man, and an impulsive man—it's hard to pin him down. Women loved him. After he killed Goliath, the women of Israel danced and sang a song in celebration of his victory.

In other words, David captured the hearts of the people. Saul's daughter, Michal, fell in love with him; Jonathan, Saul's son, became David's best friend. Even the king of the Philistines was smitten with David's charismatic personality. We will see all the sides of his personality as we move through our study of his life.

David Was a Man of National Charisma

First Samuel 18:16 is a good summary of how Israel felt about David: "But all Israel and Judah loved David, because he went out and came in before them." He was Israel personified—the focus of the hopes of the nation.

As a shepherd, he spoke to the working class; as a musician, he spoke to the artists; as a poet, he spoke to the literary group; as a king, he spoke to the leaders; as a warrior, he spoke to the military. There was something in David for everyone in the nation to love. As a result, the nation rallied together under his kingship.

DAVID WAS GREAT BECAUSE OF HIS CREATIVITY

The third way in which David was great was his creativity. It is rare today to find someone who is both a musician and an athlete, but David was. I found I had to choose between the two in college, and I chose basketball over the baritone horn. But David found time to pursue both. Seventy-three of the psalms in Israel's hymnbook (the book of Psalms) were written by David. He basically introduced hymnody to the nation of Israel on a grand scale.

If we study all the psalms of David, we find that most of them were written in response to a moment in David's life. For instance, Psalms 8, 19, and 23 were probably written during, or at least reflecting on, David's life as a shepherd. I recall being out at night once when in Canada and looking up at the tens of thousands of brilliant stars shining against the black sky and thinking about Psalm 8. In that psalm David meditates on the wonders of God's creation. I thought about how David must have contemplated the same stars while tending the sheep at night and written about God's creative hand.

David was incredibly gifted and prolific, something all of us would like to be. But like many gifted artists, David had "down" times that were as dramatic as his "up" times. And he didn't shy away from writing about both. He was honest enough to portray his walk with God in his songs exactly as it happened. Many of his psalms would be arranged in a minor key today because they reflect the dramatic and dark times of his life.

DAVID WAS GREAT BECAUSE OF THE CHOICE OF HIS LIFE

We will study more in lessons to come about how David became king, but I can summarize it at this point by saying, "God did it." God chose David to be king over Israel. How else could a young teenage boy be anointed to be the king? God pulled Saul down and set David up. David did nothing to engineer his own succession to the throne of Israel. It was all God.

There are five instances in the Scriptures that confirm this:

The Lord sought David (1 Samuel 13:14).
The Lord found David (Psalm 89:20).
The Lord chose David (Psalm 78:70).
The Lord commanded David (1 Samuel 13:14).
The Lord provided David (1 Samuel 16:1).

Five verbs—five action words—describe how clear it was that God was responsible for establishing David upon the throne of Israel. When Samuel anointed David with oil, "from that day on the Spirit of the LORD came powerfully upon David" (1 Samuel 16:13, NIV). And the next verse says that "the Spirit of the LORD had departed from Saul." God withdrew His Spirit from disobedient Saul and put that same Spirit in the heart of David.

It is the choice of David by God and the empowering of David by God's Spirit that account for David's mighty works and his greatness. We will see the hand of God at work in every chapter of David's life. From the day he felled the giant Goliath as a boy to the time he had to repent of his sins as a man, God was involved in David's life. The songs David wrote were inspired by the Spirit that dwelt in him while he accomplished the purposes of God.

DAVID WAS GREAT BECAUSE OF THE CONFESSION OF HIS LIFE

If David lived today, his sin would be the focus of the coverage of his life. His rise to prominence would only be useful as a backdrop for his fall. We are much better at telling how a person falls than we are at placing that fall in its proper context.

As I studied the life of David, I was overwhelmed by God's assessment of the man found in 1 Kings 15. There is no glossing over the failures—it is a complete assessment of all his life but with the balance that should be there. It is important to see David as a man, a human being, in order to appreciate all his giftedness and accomplishments. First Kings 15:5 says, "David did *what was* right in the eyes of the LORD, and had not turned aside from anything that He commanded him all the days of his life, except in the matter of Uriah the Hittite."

God did not focus only on David's sin, as we are prone to do. God made David's sin exactly what it was—an exception to a life that otherwise honored God. David lived a life that was centered on following God, except for the year of his involvement with Bathsheba and Uriah the Hittite. God did not cancel out all the good because of David's failure. Yes, David paid dearly for his sins, as he should have. But looking at the totality of his life, God counted his failure as an exception, not the rule.

Sometimes it is hard for us to look at a man as gifted and charismatic as David and know how we can relate to him. He seems like a man who lived on a different level from the rest of us. Not so. David was a frail human being, a man with clay feet like all of us have. And just as God does for us, He forgave David for his sins. And therein we find the secret to David's life: He was a man of confession. It is David's weakness and his spirit of confession that ties him to us; his humanity is where we find common ground with him.

If you will read Psalm 32 and Psalm 51, you will see that David was a man who learned the futility of concealing his sin. David confessed his sin, God heard his confession, and he was restored. God gave David back the joy of his salvation. It was by humbling himself before God that David's life continued to count even after he had sinned.

As you prepare to meet David in this series of lessons, prepare to meet a man like yourself—a person who wants to follow God but who has sinned. Satan would have you believe the lie that if you have failed, you are finished. That was not true for David, and it is not true for you. For David, God was the God of the second chance, and He will be that same kind of God for you. We will learn what David learned: When we confess our sins, God cleanses us from all unrighteousness (1 John 1:9).

PERSONAL QUESTIONS

1. When you picture someone who "has it all," what type of person do you envision? Does "having it all" mean a person is faultless, or that their life is uncomplicated?

2. Do you find it difficult to relate to others who seem to "have it all"? Why or why not? How might this lesson help you find common ground with everyone you meet?

3. Reviewing the context of David's life historically, why was there a dire need for a righteous leader at this time in history?

4. What type of leader was David's predecessor, Saul? Did he seem to "have it all"?

5. How does the Bible describe David's physical appearance? (1 Samuel 16:12; 17:39) His gifts? His family setting?

6. How did God view David's sin? How does God view our sins? (1 John 1:9)

7. Reflect on a time that God gave you a second chance. Then spend a moment in prayer thanking the Lord for the second chances He so mercifully extends to us each and every day.

1. Read 1 Samuel 8.

   a. Who did Samuel appoint as judges over Israel near the end of the period of the judges? (verses 1–3)

   b. What kind of leaders did they turn out to be? (verses 1–3)

   c. When the people in Israel demanded a king, what counsel did God give Samuel regarding their request? (verses 4–18)

   d. Why do you think the people still demanded a king after Samuel's warning? (verses 19–20)

   e. What danger do you see in their attitude?

   f. What type of leader did the people receive?

2. Who actually chose Saul to be king? (1 Samuel 9:17) How does the saying "Be careful what you ask God for" apply in this situation?

3. How did Israel feel about David? (1 Samuel 18:16)

4. Who established David upon the throne of Israel?

    a. Discuss the instances in the Scriptures that confirm this? (1 Samuel 13:14, 16:1; Psalm 89:20; 78:70)

5. David was born for a certain time with a specific purpose. As your group closes in prayer, ask the Lord to open your hearts to His divine direction for your lives, that you may walk in His will and "do what is right in the eyes of the Lord."

DID YOU KNOW?

When Israel demanded from Samuel that he anoint a king to rule over them, the people were saying they wanted to switch from a theocracy to a monarchy. *Theocracy* means "rule by God," whereas *monarchy* means "rule by one (*mono*) ruler or king." The Ten Commandments and other laws were a sort of constitution for Israel to govern her life as a nation. This constitution and law code was the earthly representation of the will of their heavenly King. When Israel demanded an earthly king, it became the king's responsibility to govern the nation under the same laws. Saul's failure to adhere to the constitution cost him his kingship.

MAN APPOINTS BUT GOD ANOINTS

1 Samuel 16:1–13

In this lesson we discover how God anoints for service.

OUTLINE

When we view leadership in the world, it is always about the résumé and being out front. But leadership in God's kingdom is different. It is about the heart and being a servant. David had no résumé but had the heart of a servant, so he was chosen by God to be the next king of Israel.

I. **The Responsibility for Anointing Is God's**

II. **The Requirements for Anointing Are God's**
   A. Spiritual Attitude
   B. Servant Spirit
   C. Private Person

III. **The Response to Anointing Is God's**

There is a marked difference in the selection of Saul and David as kings over Israel. Saul's choice was accompanied by the acclaim of the people because of his victories against the enemies of Israel. Remember, this was a time near the end of the period of the judges when Israel was being afflicted by neighboring nations. Like the judges before him, Saul rose up and defeated Israel's enemies, and the people rallied around him as the new king.

With David, however, it was different. Though he would become a mighty warrior later, his choice as king was the sovereign choice of God. In this lesson we will see that there is a difference between the way God chooses and the way man chooses.

THE RESPONSIBILITY FOR ANOINTING IS GOD'S

By way of reminder, the elders of Israel approached Samuel and demanded that he appoint a king to rule over Israel (1 Samuel 8:5). Samuel grieved over their demand since he knew the people were rejecting the rule of God over their lives. The defining characteristic of Saul's kingship was that it was initiated by man. Their request was a result of the hardness of their hearts. They knew better, but God granted their request and gave them what they asked for. The rise of David to the throne would be marked by completely different circumstances.

Moving ahead to 1 Samuel 16:1–3, we find the divine initiative in the selection of David. God directed Samuel to stop mourning about the loss of Saul as king and go to the house of Jesse, where he would find God's choice for the new king: "You shall anoint for Me the one I name to you." While Saul was allowed by God to become king, David was chosen to become king by God. One king was the result of man's initiative, the other the result of God's.

THE REQUIREMENTS FOR ANOINTING ARE GOD'S

First Samuel 16:6 lets us know that Samuel had an idea in mind of what the new king should look like, probably based on Saul, who was a person of stature. Samuel had a template established in his mind—which God was about to change.

As soon as Samuel saw Eliab, he thought he was looking at God's choice: "Surely the LORD's anointed *is* before Him!" But the Lord delivers the profound principle that expresses so clearly the difference between how God judges and how man judges: "Do not look at his appearance or at his physical stature, because I have refused him. For *the LORD does* not *see* as man sees; for man looks at the outward appearance, but the LORD looks at the heart" (1 Samuel 16:7).

Not only was Jesse's firstborn, Eliab, not God's choice, neither were those next in line: Abinadab, Shammah, and the remaining four. Seven sons of Jesse in all were passed in front of Samuel with God saying "No" to each one. God was apparently looking for something that could not be detected by human eyes. Samuel was looking outwardly while God was looking inwardly.

In this résumé-driven culture, everyone focuses on their outward accomplishments: education, achievements, background. You will rarely find any information about a person's heart listed on his résumé. Yet that is what God is looking for. The rest is not without some value, but what is most important to God is what is on the inside of a person. God evaluates people differently than we do. In marriage choices, business partners, employees—we need to learn to see as God sees.

There are three criteria involved in seeing and choosing the way God does.

Spiritual Attitude

We are told in 1 Samuel 13:14 that God was seeking for Himself a man after His own heart. The focus of God's selection could not be more clear: It is the heart. What does it mean to be a person after God's heart? We may never know everything that means, but at the very least we can say that whatever God loves, we love. We are people who follow after God and His heart, people who have embraced the priorities and purposes of the Almighty. Even as a young man, David apparently had this kind of heart—a heart of commitment to God and His promises.

Second Chronicles 16:9 puts God's searching process this way: "For the eyes of the LORD run to and fro throughout the whole earth, to show Himself strong on behalf of *those* whose heart *is* loyal to Him." Loyalty and commitment—those are the qualities God is looking for. And when God finds someone who is strong toward Him, He in turn is strong toward them. Some may wonder why God forgave (was strong toward) David when he sinned so grievously with Bathsheba and Uriah. It was because David was strong toward God. This doesn't mean grace and forgiveness are earned. It means that God is faithful and loyal and rewards those who are faithful and loyal toward Him.

When God looked at Jesse's sons, He saw they had pleasing exteriors, but He didn't find what He was looking for inside.

Servant Spirit

God is not looking so much for a strong spirit as He is looking for a servant spirit—a person who is a servant-leader. In Psalm 89 (not a psalm written by David), we find an interesting description of David: "Once you spoke in a vision, to your faithful people you said: 'I have bestowed strength on a warrior; I have raised up a young man from among the people. I have found David my servant; with my sacred oil I have anointed him'" (verses 19–20, NIV).

Note that God calls David "my servant," not "my strong man" or "my warrior." When Saul was chosen by the people, he had a strong spirit and many notches on his achievement belt. He stands in stark contrast to the description of David that we find in Psalm 78:70–72: "He chose David his servant and took him from the sheep pens; from tending the sheep he brought him to be the shepherd of his people Jacob, of Israel his inheritance. And David shepherded them with integrity of heart; with skillful hands he led them" (NIV). Saul went from strong to a failure, while David went from shepherd to servant. He was a servant to his sheep as a young man and became a servant to the people of Israel as their shepherd. God saw a man willing to endure the difficulties of shepherding sheep—rough terrain, wild animals, lonely vigils at night—and said, "That's the man I want to shepherd My people."

Leadership is, first of all, a matter of servanthood, at least in the biblical sense. It is not always that way in the world, and the Church has adopted more and more of the world's way of leading. Here is the world's version of leadership versus God's way:

The World's Way of Leading

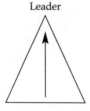

God's Way of Leading

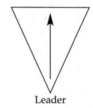

In the world, one person works his way up to the top of the triangle with everyone below him serving him. But in the kingdom of God, the servant is least of all—he is at the bottom from a spiritual point of view, serving everyone above him. The world says, "How many people are serving me?" while the biblical leader says, "How many people am I serving?"

God needed a servant-leader who would subordinate his desires to God's desires. When Saul decided to be creative by assuming the priest's duties and by altering Samuel's instruction to fit his better idea (1 Samuel 13; 15), he showed that he was more interested in serving his desires than God's.

This willingness doesn't appear on a résumé—it only appears in the heart, and only God can see the heart. We can see the manifestation of the heart over time; but when it came to choosing another king, only God could see the hearts of Jesse's eight sons. We have to be very careful when we choose people for any function, to get as clear a picture of their heart as we can.

Private Person

A third characteristic God is looking for is privacy. By that I mean a person who is not consumed with being out front in the public eye. The person may be put in such a place by God, but that is God's decision, not the person's. Many leaders God has used in this world have been plucked from obscurity by God, which is exactly where God found David. He was in the hills surrounding Bethlehem, out of public view. Like Moses, whom God called from tending sheep in Midian, David was minding his own business when God called him to a more public place.

In 1 Samuel 17 we find David recounting some of the lessons he learned while serving his sheep out of the spotlight. Saul had told David he would be no match for the Philistine giant, Goliath, but David begged to differ. He recounted how God had delivered him from the attacks of lions and bears and would surely deliver him from Goliath. Saul was impressed with what David had learned and gave him permission to battle Goliath. We know the outcome of that fight.

David got ready for the first public event of his life by being faithful in the private events of his life. Because he gained victory in his private life, he was prepared for victory when God called him into the public venues of his life. David was courageous and faithful, not because he was showing off for other people or his sheep but because it was his responsibility. Everyone who works his or her way through years of toil at seemingly insignificant jobs is developing the faithfulness needed for larger things. It is my observation after several decades of ministry that very little of what is important is public, and a great deal of what is important is private. It is our preparation in our private life that determines whether the public part of our life will have any significant, lasting impact or not. After all, when representing God in the public arena, it is only what we get from God in private that is worth anything. And if we are not spending time with God in private, then we have nothing to offer in public.

THE RESPONSE TO ANOINTING IS GOD'S

If we were writing David's story, we might have Samuel select David from among Jesse's sons, anoint him, and then take him immediately and present him to the people: "Behold, your new king!" Our desire for immediate results and fanfare always seems to go contrary to the way God works.

David was around sixteen years old when Samuel anointed him, and he became king when he was thirty—fourteen years later! During those years, David had two occupations: shepherd and fugitive. That's right—he went back to tending his sheep, probably trying to put two and two together and understand what had happened. Eventually, when he became part of Saul's court as a minstrel, and Saul became jealous of him, he had to flee for his life as a fugitive. So to prepare for being king, David had to run after sheep and run away from Saul. But we know David was filled with the Spirit on the day he was anointed by Samuel (1 Samuel 16:13), so we know his life was the life God ordered for him.

The Spirit-filled life is for the everyday moments in life, not just for being king. The apostle Paul wrote about being filled with the Spirit and then went on to talk about husbands and wives, children and their parents, servants and masters—the equivalent of tending sheep in David's day (Ephesians 5:18–6:9). In Colossians 3:16 he wrote about being filled with the Word of God "richly." Being filled with the Spirit and the Word are what we need to live in the humdrum of daily life in a way that pleases God. As the Spirit of God came upon David, He left Saul (1 Samuel 16:13–14). As Saul began to decrease, David began to increase. The presence of the Spirit and the Word are the prerequisites for effective service for God.

There are two lessons to be learned from David's preparation for kingship:

First, God is at work even when we are not aware of it. David did not know that God was looking for him while he was tending his sheep. We don't have to be aware that God is at work, but often we look back and see that He was.

Second, God does His work in a way with which we are not acquainted. God's ways are different from ours. Don't doubt that God is at work just because you don't understand what He is doing or how He is doing it.

God accomplished His sovereign purposes in David's life as a youth and gave him a larger ministry as a young adult. He did the same with Jesus, and He wants to do the same with each of us.

PERSONAL QUESTIONS

1. If someone were to describe you, do you think they would describe you as a person after God's own heart? Why or why not?

2. What type of person did Samuel have in mind when he was looking for God's choice for king? (1 Samuel 16:6) Was this description in line with the type of man God was looking for? (1 Samuel 13:14)

3. How old was David when Samuel anointed him as king? How old was he when he actually became king? What did David do during the time between these two events, and how did this prepare him for kingship?

4. Relate Luke 16:10 to the life of David. How are you fulfilling this, or not, in your own life?

5. Fill in the blanks. "The presence of the _____ and the _____ are the prerequisites for effective service for God." How can we meet these prerequisites?

6. Have you ever doubted that God was at work in your life? How can this lesson be an encouragement in moments when we don't understand God's plan?

1. What does it mean to be a man or woman after God's heart? What types of qualities does such a person possess?

2. Who appointed Saul as king? Who appointed David as king? How was God's role different in each of these situations?

3. Compare and contrast the world's way of leading with God's way of leading. Which type of leadership do we see most frequently? Why do you think this is?

4. Do you more frequently find yourself asking, "How many people are serving me?" or "How many people am I serving?" What are some practical ways you can serve those in the circles around you—friends, neighbors, family, church members, coworkers, and others?

5. What private-life experiences gave David courage as he stepped into the spotlight in the battle against Goliath? What does this teach us about the relationship between our private life and our public life?

6. Discuss ways we can gain victory in our private lives. As you close in prayer, ask God to help you draw nearer to Him and to His Word in your personal lives so that you may be prepared to serve and represent Him in the public venues of life.

DID YOU KNOW?

In the Old Testament, priests were initially anointed to designate being set apart for God's service (Exodus 29:7). But in the time of the monarchy, it was usually kings who were anointed as a sign of their having been chosen. The verb "anoint" in Hebrew was *mashach*, and one who was anointed was called *mashiach*, or "messiah." When Jesus began His ministry, He applied Isaiah 61:1 to Himself ("The Spirit of the LORD is upon Me, because He has anointed Me"—Luke 4:18), which was a clear reference to His being the Messiah of Israel. His anointing by God signified His fulfillment of all the roles of Old Testament leaders: prophet, priest, and king.

SAUL'S MOODS AND DAVID'S MUSIC

1 Samuel 16:14–23

In this lesson we learn how David received on-the-job training for his future role as king.

OUTLINE

Life is not a random series of events. Using David's life as an example, we find that his particular gifts and abilities were exactly what the ailing King Saul needed. Thus the incoming king found himself invited to serve in the court of the outgoing king, who was none the wiser.

I.   **The Intruding Spirit**

II. **The Interesting Suggestion**

III. **The Inspired Selection**

IV. **The Insignificant Servant**

V.   **The Intriguing Solution**

I n the earlier days of my pastoral ministry, I spent a week being ministered to by music. My wife had been admitted to the hospital for an undiagnosed reason and stayed there for a week while the doctors tried to determine what was wrong. I remember driving around in my car that week, listening to an Andraé Crouch tape. His song "Through It All" is what got me through that week. I almost wore that tape out because it kept reminding me to "trust in Jesus."

I can remember many other instances in my life when I was particularly discouraged or facing a challenge I did not know how to meet when God used music to quicken my spirit with faith. Music is definitely part of the Church's corporate praise and worship of God, but spiritual songs have a very personal ministry as well. Music can break through the stress and tension we live with at times and cause us to turn our faith-focus back toward God. It can't be accidental that, in the providence of God, His own hymnbook ended up right in the middle of our modern Bibles. There you will find 150 songs composed by the musicians of Israel that ministered to them and minister to us as well.

We pick up our story of David in this lesson with his preparing to minister to Saul through music. In the first half of 1 Samuel 16, David was anointed to rule; at the end of the chapter, we find him called to his first act of service. The Spirit of God has left Saul and come upon David. In place of the Spirit of God, we find a dark presence in Saul's life—the intrusion of a "distressing spirit."

THE INTRUDING SPIRIT

This is a problematic passage of Scripture since it says the "distressing spirit" was "from the LORD" (1 Samuel 16:14). To understand this, we have to go back to 1 Samuel 15 and the charge Saul was given by God to destroy the Amalekites. God commanded Saul to destroy the entire nation: men, women, children, and all the livestock. Unfortunately, Saul did not take God seriously. He spared Agag, the king of the Amalekites, and the best of the livestock (verse 9). When Samuel discovered that Saul had not carried out God's will, Saul tried to cover for himself. But eventually Saul's disobedience was made plain with this scathing condemnation from Samuel in verses 22–23:

Has the LORD *as great* delight in burnt offerings and sacrifices,
As in obeying the voice of the LORD?
Behold, to obey is better than sacrifice,
And to heed than the fat of rams.
For rebellion *is as* the sin of witchcraft,
And stubbornness *is as* iniquity and idolatry.
Because you have rejected the word of the LORD,
He also has rejected you from *being* king.

As a consequence of this judgment, God's Spirit was withdrawn and an evil spirit began to trouble Saul. It was as if the vacuum left by the departure of the Spirit of God was filled by a demonic spirit. Because we are taught as Christians that the Holy Spirit cannot be taken away from us, we have to understand why He was taken away from Saul.

Beginning at Pentecost in Acts 2, when the Holy Spirit was given as a gift to the Church, every single person who becomes a born-again Christian is permanently indwelt by the Holy Spirit. This was a new movement in God's dealings with His people. In the Old Testament, the Spirit did not permanently indwell believers. Instead, the Spirit came upon believers to empower them for service of various kinds, just as He did at first with Saul (1 Samuel 10:10; 11:6) and then later with David (1 Samuel 16:13). But sin could cause the Spirit to depart, as He did with Samson (Judges 16:20) and as David feared later in his life the Spirit might do with him (Psalm 51:11).

This cannot happen to believers today, because we live in a different period of God's work. However, during the Tribulation period yet to come upon the earth, when the Church and the indwelling Spirit have been removed from the world, the Spirit's ministry will return to that of the Old Testament. So the Spirit will selectively come upon people during that period instead of indwelling them permanently.

The literal meaning of the text describing the evil spirit and Saul is that the spirit would overwhelm him. It would come upon the king and would be as though a huge blanket of darkness had descended upon him. We have heard people use the expression, "I don't know what happened—something just came over me." That is how the evil spirit affected Saul. The king's servants were the ones who discerned the source of Saul's problem and encouraged him to find someone who could soothe his soul with music.

The Interesting Suggestion

Speaking honestly, music was not really what Saul needed. Yes, the music helped. But more than needing to be refreshed, Saul needed to repent. If they knew it was an evil spirit, they should have encouraged the king to get right with God. They did what modern healers often do today—deal with the symptoms instead of the root cause.

The Inspired Selection

When Saul's servants described David to him, they listed his qualifications (1 Samuel 16:18). First, they described him as a skilled musician. It is important when playing for the king that one be skilled—to give him the very best. The same is true for the Church today. We need to offer God the very best in music that we have.

Second, they said David was "a mighty man of valor." This translates into being a man of courage who was unafraid to take on wild animals in defending his sheep. Coupled with this was the phrase "a man of war." It may have been that David had been involved in skirmishes with the Philistines while in the fields tending his sheep. The bottom line was that David was someone who was bold and courageous.

Third, he was "prudent in speech," meaning he knew just what to say and when to say it. He was not someone the servants would be embarrassed by if they sent him to minister to the king.

Fourth, David was "a handsome person." A good way to translate the meaning of that phrase in today's language would be to say David was a sharp guy. We have already said David was charismatic; we could add to that the word "magnetic." Everyone who came in contact with David was drawn to him. Women loved him and soldiers were willing to die for him.

David was a godly man, a man after God's own heart. Reading how the servants of Saul described David raises the question: How do people think of us? Do they see us as godly persons? As people with godly qualities they could recommend to others? There is no higher compliment we can pay to another person or have another pay to us than to say, "He or she is a godly person."

What we find in David—his musical ability coupled with his godliness—is something we need more of today in the Christian music field. Musicians must be careful not to move from praise and worship and encouragement with their music to entertainment only. It is such a blessing when Christian musicians come into our churches in order to have a ministry to the Lord and to the Body of Christ rather than just using the Church as a way to promote their own ministry. I believe David must have been a musician whose godliness caused him to lift up the Lord and others through his music.

THE INSIGNIFICANT SERVANT

So Saul sent for David. The young man who had already been anointed as the king rode a donkey from Bethlehem to Gibeah, Saul's capital, carrying his lyre, a loaf of bread, a skin of wine, and taking a young goat to offer to the king—the new king was going to minister to the old king! This is a great reminder of how God uses the insignificant things in this world to accomplish His purposes: a simple shepherd boy going to minister to the king.

David was already the anointed king but demonstrated his humility and obedience to God by going to minister to Saul until the time was right to take the throne.

THE INTRIGUING SOLUTION

Like everyone who met David, Saul was mightily impressed with the young man. First Samuel 16:21 says that Saul "loved him greatly" and made David his armor bearer. Saul sent word to Jesse that he wanted David to remain in his court. And whenever the evil spirit overwhelmed Saul, David played his lyre and brought relief to the king.

We find in David a picture of the true leader serving. He stood before Saul and said, "Reporting for duty, sir." There was no resentment over having to serve one who was no longer the true king. Rather, his heart was to serve, to do whatever was asked of him.

Saul responded with love to David's willingness to serve. That is always the evidence that genuine service is taking place—it creates a bond of love between the server and the one served. When service is performed with a carnal spirit or an underlying sense of resentment, love is not the result. Love always grows out of ministry. As David served Saul with his loyalty and his music, Saul's love for David increased. This love will become evident later as Saul becomes increasingly conflicted over his own attempts to kill his young servant.

There are two truths in this chapter that are hard to miss. First, the ministry to misery is music. There is something about God's wonderful creation of the tones produced by musical instruments that has the ability to soothe a troubled soul. Music is like the alphabet. There are only 26 letters in the English language, yet they can be combined in an infinite number of ways to form what we read. Different kinds of writing inspire and minister to different people in different ways.

Likewise, there are only twelve tones in our Western musical system, but they can be combined in an infinite number of ways to create a variety of songs that minister to different people in different ways. We need to be careful not to get locked into just the music we like to the exclusion of that which others like. Chances are, the songs David played for Saul might not have been pleasing to our ears, and that cultural difference is fine. People enjoy and are helped by different kinds of music, and we must allow that to be true in the Church. That's not to say there shouldn't be standards, but we must be careful about establishing standards. We must make sure we are not imposing our preferences on others.

Standards such as the quality of lyrics—they shouldn't be debasing or degrading as are the lyrics in some popular music today—and a tempo and volume that don't overshadow the lyrics are good places to start in evaluating standards. But we must be sure not to allow our cultural preferences to assume the status of standards. What others are used to is just as valid as what we are used to.

Second, the training for leading is serving. It is interesting that when David was selected to be king, there was no leadership institute he could attend to learn how to become a king. Chasing sheep around the hillsides is not what anyone would call a leadership-training institute. Anyone except God, that is. God used David's gift of music to allow him access to the court of the king for some on-the-job training. So when it came time for David to assume the throne of Israel, he just moved a few feet over and he was there. After all, he had been serving right beside the king for a long time.

That model of training—call it the apprentice model, if you will —is the most effective way for anyone to learn to lead. The problem is that most people want to start out as the CEO instead of working in the mailroom. But David was willing to serve; as a result, he became qualified to lead.

God has given you gifts just like He did David. If you will ask Him to show you the place to begin serving, He will give you an opportunity. Whether you are moved higher or not doesn't matter. What matters is that you become qualified to lead by being willing to serve wherever God places you. Leadership is not a matter of your place on the organization chart. It is a matter of being an example and an inspiration to others.

PERSONAL QUESTIONS

1. Recall a time when you were personally ministered to by music. What was the circumstance? Was there a specific song or lyric that encouraged your heart at that time?

2. What was Saul commanded to do in 1 Samuel 15? What was Saul's response? What was the consequence of this decision?

3. Did the Holy Spirit permanently indwell believers in the Old Testament? Does the Holy Spirit permanently indwell believers today? How will the Holy Spirit indwell people during the Tribulation period yet to come upon the earth?

4. When Saul's servants described David to him, they listed his many qualifications (1 Samuel 16:18). How do others view you? Do they see you as a godly person? A person with godly qualities they could recommend to others?

5. How did Saul respond to David's willingness to serve? What is the evidence of genuine service? What cannot happen when service is performed with a carnal spirit or an underlying sense of resentment?

6. David ministered to Saul through his gift of music. What gifts has God given you that you can use to serve others? Ask the Lord for His leading in where you might be able to serve.

1. Are there any specific songs or hymns that encourage your heart in times of distress? Share with the group.

2. When the evil spirit came upon Saul, what did his servants suggest as a remedy? Was this the cure Saul needed?

3. When Saul's servants described David to him, what qualifications did they list? (1 Samuel 16:18)

   a. He was "skillful in _____."

   b. He was "a mighty _____."

   c. He was "a man of _____."

   d. He was "prudent in _____."

   e. He was a "_____ person."

4. How do you suppose others view the Church? Would you say they see believers as godly individuals? As people they could recommend to others? Why or why not?

5. When Saul sent for David, what did David do? What principles can we learn from David's response that we can apply to our own lives?

6. What was Saul's impression of David? (1 Samuel 16:21) What was David's attitude toward Saul? Had you been in David's situation, do you think you would have served Saul with the same attitude as David?

7. Complete the following sentence: "The training for leading is _____." As you close in prayer, ask God to show you a place where you can begin serving and to give you a heart that is willing to serve wherever He places you.

DID YOU KNOW?

We often see pictures and paintings of young David playing his instrument in the court of Saul, and he is shown playing the equivalent of a modern-day harp. But the ancient lyre was much smaller than a harp, small enough for David to have taken into the fields with him as he tended his sheep. It was an instrument having anywhere from three to twelve strings which were stretched over a sounding box much like a modern guitar—but without the neck. The lyre was triangular shaped and cradled in the arms when strummed or played with a plectrum (pick). Psalms 33:2; 92:3; and 144:9 may possibly refer to a lyre.

WHEN TWO GIANTS MEET

1 Samuel 17:1–38

In this lesson we learn what it takes to become a champion for God.

OUTLINE

In the spiritual life there is a balance between our part and God's part. The human tendency is to overload on our part—walking by sight—and underestimate God's part—walking by faith. David displayed the perfect balance when he set out to defeat an impossible giant named Goliath.

I. **The Challenge to the Living God**
   A. The Scene of the Challenge
   B. The Size of the Challenge
   C. The Sound of the Challenge
   D. The Seriousness of the Challenge

II. **The Champion of the Living God**
   A. He Was Consistent in the Routine of Things
   B. He Was Challenged by the Impossible Things
   C. He Was Committed in Spite of Ridicule
   D. He Was Courageous in the Lord
   E. He Was Confident in the Spirit

III. **The Conquest by the Living God**
   A. The Instruments of David
   B. The Insult to God
   C. The Intimidation of the Giant
   D. The Impact of a Champion

If you are like me, occasionally things appear on your horizon that seem larger than life, and you wonder if you are up to the challenge. Of course, the answer is "No!" In our own strength, and under our own power, we are not adequate to meet the challenges of life—even the smallest ones. But that doesn't mean we cannot conquer those giants when they appear. It means we have to defeat them the same way David defeated the biggest giant he or anyone had ever seen.

When David, still a teenager, learned there was a Philistine giant named Goliath intimidating the armies of Israel, he didn't try to tackle Goliath in his own strength. But he knew with God's strength and help Goliath could be defeated. After all, God had rescued David from the mouth of lions and bears as a shepherd. Why would God not save him from Goliath?

As we study the detailed story of David and Goliath in 1 Samuel 17, we will find principles that can be applied in our life when we face our own giants.

THE CHALLENGE TO THE LIVING GOD

This story is not so much about a teenager fighting a giant as it is the story of the ages: God being confronted by the powers of evil. This is a dramatic chapter in that story to be sure. But because it is a timeless conflict, the principles are ones any believer can apply to his or her life at any time.

The Scene of the Challenge

The stage is set in the first three verses of 1 Samuel 17. The armies of Israel and Philistia were gathered on hillsides on opposite sides of the Valley of Elah, facing one another. Bible scholars tell us the armies may not have been separated by more than a 100 yards with a ravine below them. Through the ravine would have run a small brook, the brook from which David selected his five stones (verse 40).

The Size of the Challenge

In verses 4–7 we get a detailed description of the giant Goliath. His height was the most impressive—around nine and a half feet tall. Giants were not uncommon in Canaan. When Joshua and Caleb and the other Hebrew spies went up to assess the Promised Land after coming out of Egypt, they reported seeing giants in the land—"descendants of Anak" (Numbers 13:33). But when Joshua went in to take the land, we are told that he "cut off the Anakim" (the descendants of Anak) entirely from most of the land (Joshua 11:21). But in Joshua 11:22 we read, "[the Anakim] remained only in Gaza, in Gath, and in Ashdod." And where does 1 Samuel 17:4 say Goliath was from? Gath—the very location where a pocket of the descendants of Anak remained. So Goliath was one of the remaining descendants of a family of people known for their giant stature.

To get a picture of how tall Goliath was, consider this: A regulation basketball goal stands ten feet above the floor. The top of Goliath's head would have been just a few inches beneath the rim. There have been players in the NBA as tall as seven and a half feet tall, and Goliath would have towered over them by another two feet. But he wasn't skinny like some very tall NBA players. He was proportionately big all the way around. In other words, he was a giant!

And he had weapons to fit his size: a giant brass helmet, a coat of armor that weighed between 150 and 200 pounds, a huge spear with a metal point that weighed between fifteen and twenty pounds (just the metal point!), brass armor on his legs, and a man going in front of him carrying his shield. They probably needed the strongest and tallest man in the Philistine army just to carry Goliath's shield.

The Sound of the Challenge

Goliath came out of the Philistine camp and taunted the armies of Israel (verses 8–10). The challenge Goliath made was economical: "Why waste all our soldiers in battle—the victor will have no servants after it's all over. Let's have one person from each side represent each army and settle this thing neatly. Whichever man wins, his army will become servants of the other army." That challenge was easy for Philistia to make—after all, they had Goliath. Israel had not sent anyone out to represent them because they had no one who could possibly defeat Goliath.

The Seriousness of the Challenge

Verse 16 tells us that Goliath's taunting had been going on for forty days, and all that time no one from Israel's side had stepped out to accept the challenge. Israel was scared to death, quivering in their sandals (verse 11).

Consider the time frame—six weeks. You have no doubt been through a financial, medical, relational, or other situation that lasted that long, or longer. Every day you are taunted by the situation, and you live in fear of stepping out to meet it head-on. Pretty soon it begins to dominate your life. It is the first thing you think of in the morning and the last thing you think of at night—and you probably dream about it as well.

That is the way it was with Goliath. At all hours of the day and night, his challenge echoed through the Valley of Elah. And Israel was silenced by their fear. All of Israel, that is, except for a teenager named David.

THE CHAMPION OF THE LIVING GOD

I believe the hearts of champions are the same regardless of the age or endeavor. Whether it's David on the battlefield or a great champion in athletics, medicine, business, ministry, or the family, the heart of a champion always displays consistent characteristics. And we see them all in David.

He Was Consistent in the Routine of Things

Beginning in 1 Samuel 17:12, we are introduced to David. Three of his older brothers, Eliab, Abinadab, and Shammah, were with the Israelite army; David was in Bethlehem tending his father's sheep. David apparently moved back and forth between Saul's headquarters in Gibeah and his home in Bethlehem a few miles away (verse 15). With Saul at war, there would have been no need for David to be with the king. David was the king-in-waiting, but he was comfortable fulfilling his assigned roles until the time came to ascend to the throne.

David was sent by his father, Jesse, to take food to his three brothers. So in addition to being the king's musician and his father's shepherd, he now becomes an errand boy for his brothers (verse 20). Jesse was old at this point and dependent on David to manage things with his sheep (verse 12). It is worth noting that before leaving Bethlehem, David "left the sheep with a keeper" (verse 20). Even in the little things, David was faithful and responsible.

Champions focus on details. I heard an athletic coach once say that it's not hard to find people who have the desire to win, but it is hard to find people who have the desire to prepare to win. David was one who was willing. David seems to have been consistently faithful in the routine matters of life, preparing himself well for what was to come.

When the apostle Paul described David, he used God's words: ". . . a man after My *own* heart, who will do all My will" (Acts 13:22). David was a man who was willing to carry out the will of God, which meant carrying out the will of those in authority over him, whether it was the king or his father. Champions are consistent in the routines of life.

He Was Challenged by the Impossible Things

Just as David arrived at the Israelite army camp and found his brothers to give them the food from Jesse, Goliath made an appearance in the Valley of Elah. When Goliath came out, all the Israelite soldiers fled back to the camp, leaving David to contemplate this unusual situation: one man intimidating an entire army. David discovered the situation and also discovered that Saul had offered a reward for whoever could kill Goliath: cash, the king's daughter in marriage, and exemption from taxes for the family of the victor.

We need to note that Saul was willing to fund his own fear. He stood head and shoulders above the rest of the army—he should have been out there fighting Goliath as the leader of the army. But because the Spirit of God had departed from Saul, he was operating in the flesh—and scared to confront the giant. As we will see, the absence of the Spirit in Saul and the presence of the Spirit in David is what made the difference between the two.

But before David could get to Saul to volunteer to fight Goliath, he had to overcome the ridicule of others.

He Was Committed in Spite of Ridicule

Champions are always ridiculed by those who are too afraid or too weak to be champions themselves. If you want to be a champion for God, you will be criticized. The main person to attack David was Eliab, his older brother. Remember that Eliab was the first one Samuel had identified as God's choice to be king. But Eliab was passed over and David, his little brother, was chosen. There was clearly some lingering resentment in Eliab that came out as he attacked David's courage.

David had to decide whether to fight his critic or fight the true giant. Champions never lose sight of the goal; they always keep their eye on the ball, regardless of what their critics say. David reminded his brother and others who attacked him that he was not the problem—Goliath was (verse 29). In other words, "Guys, let's stay focused on the real problem."

Word got to Saul about David's presence in the camp, and David volunteered to fight Goliath. And David received the same criticism from Saul as from his brothers. All of them were cowards. They were criticizing David in order to cover up their own cowardice, something champions always have to face. If the soldiers had been servants of God, like David, instead of servants of Saul, they would have seen things differently.

He Was Courageous in the Lord

In verses 34–37 we see David's courage emerge. In defending himself against his critics' attacks, David did not brag on himself but on God. He gave credit to God for having been with him in previous challenges in his life. He was strong in the Lord, not in himself.

He Was Confident in the Spirit

In verse 38 we see David trying to put on Saul's armor at Saul's insistence; when he did, he couldn't even move. Remember, Saul was tall—his armor would have swallowed David. So he graciously declined the offer. After all, he wasn't going to meet Goliath in man's strength but in God's. He didn't need the kind of armor Saul was used to depending on. David was confident in the Spirit of God, not in man's weapons of war.

THE CONQUEST BY THE LIVING GOD

Finally, David faced his foe and was victorious through faith in the living God.

The Instruments of David

We find in verse 40 what David chose instead of Saul's weapons and armor: a staff, his sling, and five smooth stones. Clearly, this victory would be God's if it occurred.

The Insult to God

In verses 41–44, we find Goliath ridiculing the challenger the Israelites have sent forth: a boy wearing no armor and carrying no sword or spear! Goliath sneered and mocked David and cursed him in the name of his gods, one of which was Dagon, the Philistine god that couldn't stay on its pedestal in the presence of the ark of the covenant (1 Samuel 5:2–7). David would have been aware of this story and probably chuckled inside since Dagon was who Goliath was depending on for help.

The Intimidation of the Giant

David turned the tables and intimidated the giant in the name of the God of Israel (verses 45–47). As Goliath drew near, David slung a single stone that hit Goliath in the forehead and killed him instantly. He then took Goliath's own sword and lopped off the head of the giant, just to make sure the deed was completely done. The Philistines uttered a collective "Uh-oh" and headed for the hills with the (now courageous) Israelites in hot pursuit.

God used a foolish thing—a boy with a sling—to confound the wise and the mighty.

The Impact of a Champion

If we are going to be champions like David, we will have to do what he did:

1. Confront our problems. They don't just go away, and we cannot pass them off to someone else.
2. Cherish our trophies. We must depend today on the fact that God has given us victories in the past.
3. Concentrate on our goals. Don't be distracted by critics. We must stay focused on God and His ability to give us victory.

PERSONAL QUESTIONS

1. Have you ever come up against a challenge you felt you could not face in your own strength? What was your response?

2. When Goliath challenged the armies of Israel, what was their response? Why did no one come forth to fight Goliath? (1 Samuel 17:11) Where were David's brothers at this time? (verses 13–14) Where was David at this time? (verse 15)

3. Who ridiculed David for his willingness to fight Goliath? How did David defend himself against his critics?

4. Why didn't David require the protection of Saul's armor? In whom did David find his confidence? (1 Samuel 17:34–37)

5. How did David ultimately defeat Goliath? (1 Samuel 17:48–51)

6. Read 2 Corinthians 10:3–5. Explain in your own words how Paul's philosophy of spiritual battle parallels that of David's.

7. What spiritual armor is available to the Christian to face the challenges in his or her own life? (Ephesians 6:14–17)

8. If we want to be champions like David, we will have to:

    a. _____ our problems.

    b. _____ our trophies.

    c. _____ our goals.

    Ask the Lord to help you take these steps and gain victory over the "giants" in your own life.

GROUP QUESTIONS

1. What are some examples of modern-day "giants" we might face in our daily lives? This can include any type of challenge or personal struggle members of your group may be facing.

2. How do the Scriptures describe Goliath? Where was Goliath from? Why is this significant? (1 Samuel 17:4–7; Numbers 13:33; Joshua 11:22)

3. With what types of armor was Goliath equipped? (1 Samuel 17:5–7)

4. What were the terms of Goliath's challenge? Why wouldn't the rest of the army take part in this battle? (1 Samuel 17:8–10) For how many days did Goliath's taunting of Israel's army go on? (1 Samuel 17:16)

5. When David volunteered to fight Goliath, why didn't he accept Saul's armor? (1 Samuel 17:38–39) Which weapons and armor did David choose instead? (1 Samuel 17:40)

6. How does the Christian know when he or she should take up a sling versus a sword and shield? Is there a rule to follow? Or is every situation different?

7. As you close in prayer, ask the Lord for courage to confront the giants in your own life, not relying on your own strength but upon His.

DID YOU KNOW?

When David faced the giant Goliath, there was more at stake than the pride of victory. David didn't know it yet, but he would learn that his throne would be established forever and become the throne of Israel's Messiah. Should he have been killed in his contest with Goliath, there would have been no throne of David or the Son of David (1 Kings 2:45; Matthew 9:27). "Son of David" was a commonly used title among Jews for the coming Messiah (Matthew 12:23; 20:30; 21:9; 22:41–45), and Matthew began his genealogy of Christ by referring to Him as "the Son of David, the Son of Abraham" (Matthew 1:1).

THE HIGH COST OF SUCCESS

1 Samuel 17:55–18:16

In this lesson we discover what can accompany success in life.

OUTLINE

Most people don't worry about how to handle fame and fortune—but they should. Everyone experiences victories and successes along the way, even if they are small ones. Success reveals a person's true character: either humility and gratitude or pride and presumption.

I. **David's Success Created a New Family**

II. **David's Success Created a New Fame**

III. **David's Success Created a New Foe**

IV. **David's Success Created a New Friend**

I f you are a sports enthusiast like myself, you might know the answer to this question: What do Red Auerbach, Vince Lombardi, Casey Stengel, and John Wooden have in common? Besides the fact that they are all famous coaches, they are among the rare breed of coaches who won back-to-back championships in their respective sports. While it is extremely difficult to be a champion even once, it is even more difficult to be a champion two or more times in successive years. It is a life-changing experience; it puts one in a whole new league.

That is what happened to David, the shepherd boy, when he killed the Philistine giant, Goliath. For the first time in his life, he would begin to experience the pressures that accompany public fame. There is a very important phrase that occurs three times, describing how David acted. Following the NIV translation, the phrase refers to David's "success" in the days following his fight with Goliath (1 Samuel 18:5, 14–15, 30). The Hebrew verb means "to act wisely or prudently," and the contemporary term "success" incorporates that image nicely.

Few people can handle the fame and fortune that accompany great victories in life, but David did it successfully—with wisdom and skill.

DAVID'S SUCCESS CREATED A NEW FAMILY

The last few verses of 1 Samuel 17, covering David's defeat of Goliath and Saul's reaction, can be confusing. It appears that Saul does not know who David is—although he had just spoken to him a few verses earlier, and David had also been in the king's presence playing music for him. The best way to view this text is as a literary flashback covering comments made by Saul to his military commander, Abner, as David was going down to meet Goliath. Saul does not want to know who David is. Rather, he wants to know about David's family: "'Abner, whose son *is* this youth?' . . . 'Inquire whose son this young man *is*.' . . . 'Whose son *are* you, young man?'" (verses 55–58) The emphasis is obviously on David's father, not David. David's answer was, "I *am* the son of your servant Jesse the Bethlehemite."

Why was this important to Saul? It had to do with the reward Saul had promised to the man who killed Goliath: his daughter's hand in marriage and tax exemption for his father's house (verse 25). His interest in David had to do with these rewards—he was about to become an in-law of David and David's father.

Another reason is found in 1 Samuel 18:2: Saul "would not let [David] go home to his father's house anymore," and Jesse needed to be notified. Saul intended to make David a permanent part of his royal court as opposed to the part-time role he had played heretofore. David had been conscripted to the king's service. David's life was about to change in four distinct ways: he would have plenty of money from his reward, a new wife, no taxes to pay, and permanent residence in the king's palace. The solitude of the hillsides was to be replaced by a busy and public life with Saul. These are the kinds of sudden changes that have destroyed many a lesser man.

DAVID'S SUCCESS CREATED A NEW FAME

Not only did David now have a new family, he had a new fame. We learn in verses 5–7 that, on their way back to Gibeah, crowds came out to greet Saul and his entourage. Women were dancing and singing, "Saul has slain his thousands, and David his ten thousands." Overnight, David had become the subject of a new song of celebration. He was a hero, his name a household word. Just a day before, no one knew who David, the son of Jesse, was. Those who did know him knew only that he was a shepherd who tended his father's sheep, like thousands of other young men scattered throughout Israel.

Remember, "David" does not appear in the Bible as a name before David, the son of Jesse. So it was not a common name in Israel at all. But now this "beloved one" was hearing his name spoken wherever he went: "David, the giant killer." Note how he was accepted:

- Verse 5: Saul's servants and the population at large loved him.
- Verse 16: All Israel and Judah loved him.
- Verse 30: David was more successful than all of Saul's servants, and his name was highly esteemed.

David's life was no longer his own. In modern terms, the paparazzi would've followed his every move, taking pictures and reporting his whereabouts. Charles Haddon Spurgeon spoke of the problem of popularity in his writings noting that success often exposes a man to the pressure of people and thus tempts him to hold on to his gains "by means of fleshly methods and practices."

Success can be like an addictive drug: the more one takes, the more one has to have to keep the buzz going. Success can stimulate greed and ambition so that one remains at the pinnacle. As others succeed, it takes more to beat them and to stay on top. The battle for success can consume a person like a wasting disease.

Apparently, this did not happen to David. George Whitfield, the eighteenth-century English evangelist, said when some of his friends came to warn him of the danger of popularity: "I thank you heartily. May God reward you for watching over my soul. And as to what my enemies say against me, why I know worse things about myself than they've ever said." Whitfield knew himself too well to be impressed with himself.

DAVID'S SUCCESS CREATED A NEW FOE

But not everyone was in love with David. The very man whom David caused to look good in the eyes of the people for defeating the Philistines, King Saul, was raging with jealousy toward David. When Saul disobeyed the Lord in dealing with the Amalekites, Samuel prophesied that the kingdom of Israel would be torn from Saul and given "to a neighbor of yours, *who is* better than you" (1 Samuel 15:28). Perhaps Saul had come to realize who that neighbor was—a teenage shepherd! And he wasn't happy about it. Indeed, in 1 Samuel 18:8 Saul, in his frustration, says, "They have ascribed to David ten thousands, and to me they have ascribed *only* thousands. Now *what* more can he have but the kingdom?" He knew it was only a matter of time before he was out and David was in.

From that day on, Saul began a serious decline. He began to act completely irrationally as he attempted to remove David from the scene by either killing him himself or having him killed. He was jealous, fearful, and suspicious of David's motives. He actually threw a spear at David twice to try to kill him (verses 10–11). Finally, Saul's hatred of David became so intense that he became David's enemy "continually" (verse 29). The one man who had benefited the most from David's life through his musical talent suddenly found himself the enemy of David.

Sometimes those who find themselves in the middle of success discover that people who used to be their friends have become their enemies as a result of jealousy and envy. That is what happened to David's friend King Saul.

David's sudden rise in popularity would have been a challenge for anyone, even a spiritual person. But we have to remember that Saul was operating in a natural, carnal state. In verse 12 we are told that Saul was afraid because the Lord had left him. The word for "afraid" actually means "apprehensive." Saul was watching David out of the corner of his eye whenever he was around. In verse 15 Saul was again "afraid"; but this time, the word means "in awe." Saul had a hard time understanding how this young man had begun to overshadow him so quickly. And in verse 29 there is another reference to Saul's fear—but this time he was "still more afraid." Apprehension became awe, which led to fear, which led to Saul becoming David's enemy.

DAVID'S SUCCESS CREATED A NEW FRIEND

Fortunately, with a new enemy rising on David's horizon, he gained a new friend as well. We've all heard of friends who stick with us when times get hard, but I believe just as valuable a friend is the one who sticks by you when things are really good and all your other friends have succumbed to jealousy and envy.

David's friend was Jonathan, the son of Saul, as described in verses 1–4. The days surrounding David's victory over Goliath must have been difficult ones for Jonathan, having seen his father succumb to fear for six weeks in the face of Goliath and then be shown up by a teenager who went out and killed the giant with a sling and a stone. Jonathan must have been in pain for his father, yet truly excited about the new warrior who went out in the power of God to defeat the enemy. This was a new day in Israel, and Jonathan was as enamored with David as everyone else was in Israel and Judah.

Jonathan proved to be a valuable friend to David, a buffer between David and his own father who was trying to take David's life. What a difficult position this was for Jonathan! Yet he appears to have loved both his father and David and to have acted honorably toward both. We do not know if Jonathan knew about David's anointing to be king, but if he did, he showed no bitterness over his own loss of the throne. Everyone should have at least one friend like Jonathan who will stick by him when times are good and when times are bad.

There are two factors that explain how and why David was able to be wise and skilled in handling his overnight celebrity status in Israel.

First, David refused to be changed by his success. David was the same person after defeating Goliath as he was before. Whatever his father had told him to do before that contest, he did. Whatever Saul told him to do after that contest, he did. He was obedient and submissive to authority, never assuming he was too big or smart to do what he was assigned to do. Sometimes success makes us think we are too good to associate with "the little people," too good to deal with the everyday things in life. The day after killing Goliath, David was right back where he had been before: playing music on his lyre to soothe the soul of the king. David didn't think his victory granted him any special status—and he was right. He didn't ask for all the fame and fortune that came his way, nor did he do anything to deserve Saul's hatred. It appears that David put his trust in the Lord and did not fret because of evildoers (Psalm 37:1, 8).

Second, David refused to take credit for his success. To put it another way, David was "underwhelmed" with himself. When David went out to battle Goliath, he did not go out in David's name—he went out in the Lord's name. And we have to believe that when the women were singing and dancing and praising David's name, he was probably embarrassed by all the attention. David seemed to know that his success was due to the Lord being with him (1 Samuel 18:14). David is an example of the truth that there is no limit to how far we can go if we don't care who gets the credit. Or, more specifically, if we return the credit to God.

No one who suddenly achieves fame decides to ruin their life by becoming self-absorbed, but it does happen. Little by little they start reading and believing all the press; then, one day, they wake up a different person. Perhaps in the beginning that person was humble and thankful to God, and now he is taking credit for all his good fortune. When that kind of pride sets in, that person should be prepared for a fall (James 4:6).

Most of us will never have to deal with the kind of success David enjoyed. But we all enjoy victories here and there. Our goal should be to remain like David: faithful, humble, and conscious that God gets the credit.

1. When someone around you succeeds, are you more prone to feel jealous or to rejoice with the person who has succeeded?

2. When David began to experience the pressures that accompany public fame, how did he behave? (1 Samuel 18:5, 14–15, 30)

3. How did the people react to David's success? (1 Samuel 18:5–7, 16, 30) How did Saul react to David's fame? (1 Samuel 18:8)

4. Of what is jealousy a sign or evidence? (1 Corinthians 3:3) If one finds jealousy, what else might one expect to find? (2 Corinthians 12:20) Was this true in King Saul's life?

5. What two factors explain how and why David was able to be wise in handling his fame in Israel? Fill in the blanks.

   a. David refused to be _____ by his success. How did David's attitude before defeating Goliath compare to his attitude afterward?

   b. David refused to _____ for his success. Did David care about receiving credit for his success?

6. What parts of David's rise, or Saul's fall, can you personally identify with? What lessons have you learned in your life about the dangers of success?

1. What kinds of success in others' lives do you think people are most likely tempted to be jealous or envious of? Why do you think this is?

2. In what four distinct ways did David's life change after he defeated Goliath? (1 Samuel 17:25)

3. What impact did David's success have on Saul? (1 Samuel 18:15) How did this lead to Saul becoming David's enemy?

4. What can we learn from this lesson about the effects of jealousy on our relationships with others?

5. Read Romans 13:13. With what other kinds of carnal actions does Paul include jealousy? What does this say about its seriousness?

6. What is not present if envy is present? (1 Corinthians 13:4) What does Peter say to do with jealousy if we find it in ourselves? (1 Peter 2:1) Discuss ways we can do this.

7. David responded to his success with wisdom and skill. As you close, pray for wisdom for the members of your group—both in dealing with personal successes and responding to the successes of others.

DID YOU KNOW?

The idea of a bride and groom exchanging gifts and vows with one another is rooted in ancient traditions of covenant-making and -keeping. When David and Jonathan entered into a covenant with one another, Jonathan gave David his robe, his tunic, and his weapons of war (1 Samuel 18:1–4). That was a way of saying, "All my possessions are yours. By giving you my sword, I pledge myself to defend you. Anyone who attacks you attacks me as well." They also exchanged vows as covenant friends. Jonathan told David he would do anything for him that he needed (1 Samuel 20:4).

THE FUGITIVE

1 Samuel 18:17–19:24

In this lesson we discover what can accompany success in life.

OUTLINE

Insurance is supposed to protect us against loss. But there are some losses for which there is no earthly protection. When we lose hope, courage, even friends, it is better to have blessed assurance than the best insurance. This is what David discovered when he lost everything.

I. **When You Know God's Promises, You Don't Have to Prove Anything**

II. **When You Know God's Faithfulness, You Don't Have to Fear Anything**

III. **When You Know God's Fellowship, You Can Handle Losing a Friend**

OVERVIEW

There is a clear danger in the Church today of adopting many of the world's ideas. Certain kinds of humanistic and New Age thinking have made their way into pulpits and books that Christians read, especially those dealing with human potential and positive mental attitude philosophy—the "If You Can Conceive It, You Can Achieve It" philosophy. There is certainly nothing wrong with being oriented toward success and working hard to achieve what we can in life. But such thinking can become totally self-oriented if we are not careful. We can begin to use God to help us achieve our goals instead of centering our lives on His goals for our life.

These are not new philosophies. Man through the ages has found his own ego to be in competition with the Spirit of God. The Spirit and the flesh are enemies of one another (Galatians 5:17). There is a fine line that divides our desire to do all we can for God and our willingness to allow God to do all He can for us. Keeping our part and God's part in balance is a daily quest. David experienced this pressure, and we find it increasing in the period following his great victory over Goliath. God led David into a number of situations designed to purge him of his dependence on self, to help him realize that he had to learn to depend on God first.

We have followed the progression of David's life after meeting Saul. All was well until David's victory over Goliath, after which Saul's jealousy of David turned into hatred. Ultimately, "Saul became David's enemy continually" (1 Samuel 18:29). When we come to 1 Samuel 19, we find Saul's murderous spirit still active against David—he tried a third time to kill him with a spear (1 Samuel 18:10–11; 19:10). When that failed, he sent men to David's house to try to kill him, and David was forced to escape through a window (19:11–12).

So now David is a fugitive. He must now live with a completely different kind of pressure than he experienced when he faced Goliath. That pressure was just one moment in time; now he faces the pressure of being sought and killed every moment of every day. In this time of his life, David learned three major lessons that God wants to teach all who are learning to depend on Him.

When You Know God's Promises, You Don't Have to Prove Anything

David went through a very exhausting and unnecessary process of trying to prove himself worthy of becoming King Saul's son-in-law. Instead of standing on the promise of God—that he was the newly-anointed king—David was still struggling to accept himself the way God had accepted him. Here's what happened:

In 1 Samuel 18:17, Saul promised his daughter Merab to David on the condition that he continue to fight Saul's battles for him. (Saul assumed David would be killed in the process and his troubles with the young hero would be over.) David, however, said he wasn't worthy of the king's daughter, so Merab was given to another. But another of Saul's daughters, Michal, was in love with David; so Saul offered her to David on the condition that he kill 100 Philistines as a dowry. David still considered himself unworthy of the king's daughter but agreed to the marriage.

However, in order to impress King Saul—the same king who had already tried to kill him with a spear—David went out and killed 200 Philistine warriors instead of 100. Again, Saul's intent in this exercise was for David to be killed. But David, being the valiant and trustworthy warrior that he was, survived his encounters with the Philistines and brought back the evidence of the dowry to Saul. He doubled the dowry as a means of proving to himself and to Saul that he was indeed worthy of marrying the king's daughter.

We have to ask, "Why?" Why was David so intent on proving his worth to Saul? We read in 1 Samuel 16 that Samuel had taken the oil of anointing and gone to Bethlehem and anointed David as the new king of Israel. David was the king, and here he was groveling in self-induced unworthiness before a man who was trying to kill him, saying, "I'm not worthy!" David's big mistake at this point in his young life was trying to prove something that God had already promised.

As those who belong to God, we do not work and live and serve *for* acceptance. Rather, we work and live and serve *from* acceptance. I do not work to try to prove my worthiness to God, but I work to live out the fact that God has accepted me in Christ. God has accepted me in His Son because of what He did, not because of what I did. I have nothing to prove, but I do have something to practice: my acceptance into the family of God. I do not work for acceptance but from acceptance.

This is the theme of Paul's letter to the Ephesians. The first three chapters demonstrate that we have been accepted by God in Christ, and the last three chapters explain what it means to "walk worthy of the calling with which you were called" (Ephesians 4:1). Note these words: "walk worthy of the calling." Because God has called us to Himself in Christ, we are worthy. It is not our job to prove our worthiness but to walk in it.

This flies in the face of teachings of human potential, positive self-image, and self-esteem. We don't need to work for better self-esteem—we have already been esteemed by God as worthy in Christ. We can't have any higher esteem than that.

We admire David's courage and humility, but he was operating from the wrong premise with Saul. Once God has made a promise, we have nothing to prove.

When You Know God's Faithfulness, You Don't Have to Fear Anything

We also find that David wavers back and forth in his faith, just as we sometimes do. At one point he is the epitome of courage; at another point, he is filled with fear. He believes one thing but is living another.

In Psalm 59 we find a piece of information about this period in David's life. At the very beginning of almost every psalm is a note that was part of the original Hebrew text of the psalm. Often it is a musical note, and sometimes it includes information about the setting of the psalm. In Psalm 59 we find this inscription: "A Michtam [type of song] of David when Saul sent men, and they watched the house in order to kill him." This psalm was written by David during the period of David's life we are now studying—when Saul sent men to his house to kill him.

Back in 1 Samuel 19, we find that Saul has ordered his son Jonathan, who has become David's covenant friend, and other men to kill David. But Jonathan intervened and convinced Saul not to harm David, and "[David] was in [Saul's] presence as in times past" (verse 7).

But then war with the Philistines erupted again, and David went out and won a great victory against them. Saul reacted just as he had before, with jealousy and a murderous spirit—he tried to kill David the third time with a spear. David escaped the attack and fled into the night. He returned to his house and to his wife, Michal, while Saul's men were sent to watch David's house in order to kill him. As I mentioned earlier, Michal helped David escape through a window. When Saul's men arrived, Michal convinced them David was sick—she had arranged David's bed to make it appear he was in the bed asleep. But Saul insisted that his men bring him anyway, and they discovered it was a ruse—that Michal had helped David escape. When Saul confronted his daughter Michal, she lied, saying David had threatened to kill her if she did not aid his escape.

This became a very confusing situation for David. A few weeks earlier, he had faced a nine-foot giant with nothing but a sling and a stone and the power of Almighty God. With just the faithfulness of God, he had the courage to defeat his enemy. He showed no fear whatsoever as he faced the one who was trying to harm him. Now David faced a lying wife and a few soldiers and a deluded king, and his faith was replaced by fear. He was not acting in accord with his beliefs.

Returning to Psalm 59, we see what David really believed. I encourage you to read this entire psalm, and you'll see how perfectly it fits with the circumstances in 1 Samuel 19. But it also raises the question, "How could David seem so committed to trusting God in Psalm 59 and then act with such fear and deceit in 1 Samuel 19?" And then we wonder what he should have done. Should he have stayed in his house and let Saul capture him, believing that God would protect him?

These are not easy questions, but we see that God did do an amazing thing for David as the story unfolds. David fled from his house to Ramah to see Samuel. So Saul sent three groups of his soldiers to Ramah to capture David; each time, the Spirit of God came upon the men and they began prophesying! So Saul went himself, and the same thing happened to him—the Spirit of God came upon him. Saul "stripped off his clothes and prophesied before Samuel in like manner, and lay down naked all that day and all that night" (verse 24). Amazing! Saul was transformed from a murderer into a prophet. While Saul and his soldiers were distracted by the Spirit, David left and returned to Jonathan.

So God did intervene for David without the use of lies or deception. We never know what God will do or how He will intervene. We do not need to resort to the ways of the world, the "counsel of the ungodly" (Psalm 1:1), in order to accomplish God's purposes. David was learning that God would be his support system if he would only let Him. Does God ever use human means of intervention? Yes. But the challenge of the godly and mature saint is to keep our focus and our actions completely consistent with God and His ways and not succumb to the ways of the world.

WHEN YOU KNOW GOD'S FELLOWSHIP, YOU CAN HANDLE LOSING A FRIEND

The last lesson David is going to learn is that if God is all he has, that is still enough for any and every situation.

Think of what David had lost. He lost his relationship with Saul, and he apparently lost his relationship with his wife, Michal (who appears again later, in 2 Samuel, as contemptuous as ever). And now we discover he even loses contact with Jonathan. They part on good terms, but as David flees from Saul, he loses touch with the only person who has been his friend.

Jonathan continued to try to get his father, the king, to stop pursuing David. And Jonathan and David devised a plan whereby Jonathan would let David know of Saul's intent. In 1 Samuel 20:41–42 we find Jonathan and David swearing friendship to one another as they go their separate ways. Jonathan goes back to Saul, and David flees from Saul.

In Psalm 63 we find the inscription, "A Psalm of David when he was in the wilderness of Judah." David found himself thirsting for God "in a dry and thirsty land where there [was] no water" (Psalm 63:1). God had removed everything from David's life that he might have depended on and was teaching him to depend solely on Him. This was a terrible time in David's life, as it is in any of our lives when we are alone in the world with no resources and no friends. But even in those moments—as David was discovering and as we can discover—if we have God, we have enough.

We would always prefer the easier way, but as these verses point out, God knows best how to handle our requests:

I asked of God that He should give success
To the high task I sought for Him to do.
I asked that every hindrance might grow less,
And that my hours of weakness might be few.

I asked that far and lofty heights be scaled,
And now I humbly thank Him that I failed.
For with the pain and sorrow came to me,
A dower of tenderness in act and thought,

With the failure came a sympathy
An insight which success had never brought.
Father, I had been foolish and unblessed
If Thou hadst granted me my blind request.

—Author Unknown

God's promises, faithfulness, and fellowship will always be enough to meet our need and see us through.

PERSONAL QUESTIONS

1. Have you ever felt unworthy? What was the circumstance?

2. When Saul promised his daughter Merab to David, why did David decline his offer?

3. When David agreed to marry Saul's daughter Michal, how many Philistine warriors did he agree to kill as a dowry? How many Philistine warriors did he actually kill? What was David's motivation in doing this?

4. What was Saul's intent in sending David out to kill the Philistine warriors? Was Saul's plan successful?

5. Why was David so intent on proving his worth to Saul? What promise did he have from God? Had David accepted himself the way God had accepted him?

6. To what degree do you struggle with trying to prove yourself to God?

7. Why don't Christians need to work for acceptance from God? (Ephesians 2:8) What are we to do instead? (Ephesians 4:1)

8. What are the three major lessons we can take away from this chapter about depending on God? Fill in the blanks.

   a. When you know God's _____, you don't have to _____ anything.

   b. When you know God's _____, you don't have to _____ anything.

   c. When you know God's _____, you can handle _____ a friend.

GROUP QUESTIONS

1. What does it mean to truly depend on someone? What makes a person dependable? Why do we sometimes prefer to depend on ourselves rather than on others?

2. Which statement more frequently describes your response in times of trouble: "I depend on myself" or "I depend on God"? Why is this? If comfortable, share with the group.

3. During the period of David's life we are now studying, David learned three major lessons. Discuss the following circumstances and the lessons we can take away from each:

   a. David became intent on proving his worth to Saul. Why didn't David need to prove his worthiness? What was the subsequent lesson?

   b. When Saul's men came to David's house in order to kill him, how did David escape? Do you think he was depending on himself or on God? When Saul sent three groups of his soldiers to Ramah to capture David, how did God intervene? What was the subsequent lesson?

c. When David found himself with no resources and no friends, on whom did he depend? What was the subsequent lesson?

4. If time permits, encourage one another by sharing examples of times when you, or someone you know, have depended on God and He met the need.

DID YOU KNOW?

After Martin Luther nailed his *95 Theses* to the door of the church in Wittenberg, Germany, in 1517, he became a wanted man. Some of his friends hid him in a fortress overlooking the Rhine River to protect him. After being sequestered only a short time, he wrote to his friend Philipp Melanchthon, expressing his fear that all was lost. He decided to leave the fortress and enter the mainstream of life and trust God with his protection. Not long after, he wrote the now famous hymn "A Mighty Fortress Is Our God." Luther decided to entrust himself to the "bulwark never failing" to protect him from those seeking to do him harm.

REACHING AN ALL-TIME LOW

1 Samuel 21–22

In this lesson we learn how to avoid making decisions we will regret.

OUTLINE

A common assumption among mature Christians is that they have the mind of the Lord—that they can act without first seeking God's guidance. That's an assumption that doesn't always hold up. The best way to avoid bad consequences stemming from bad choices is to seek the Lord.

I. **David Defiled Before Ahimelech**

II. **David Degraded Before Achish**

III. **David Delivered Before Adullam**

IV. **Applications**
   A. When You Are Out of Fellowship With God, You Seek Bad Counsel
   B. When You Are Out of Fellowship With God, You Select Bad Choices

I knew of a man who had done great things for the Lord, founding ministries and funding them with his own money. He was a successful businessman and a pillar in his community. But financial difficulty came his way, and he became desperate for money. He took out a large life insurance policy on his wife and contracted with some criminals to have her killed in order to collect the insurance payout. When I heard about this, I thought there must be some mistake—but there wasn't. This man is currently serving time in prison for this crime.

Some say a Christian couldn't do such a thing. But it is possible. In this lesson we will see how a saint as valiant as David fell to depths he himself might not have considered possible. And it is possible for any believer today to do the same if we allow ourselves to become detached from Christ. Through the years, I have seen Christians do things to themselves and to others that I would not have believed if I hadn't witnessed them. That is why I can read the story of David and take from it the firm warning that anyone is only a decision away from falling.

David is a man who is working out his faith with fear and trembling. His behavior doesn't always match his beliefs. He can pen glorious words of trust in a psalm and then flee from a situation in abject fear for his life. In that regard, we are at times very much like David—strong on Sunday but weak on Monday.

We left David as he parted from his covenant friend Jonathan and fled to a place called Nob. From there it was a downhill journey into difficulty.

DAVID DEFILED BEFORE AHIMELECH

The first person David encountered in the small village of Nob, just north of Jerusalem, was a priest named Ahimelech. This was a sleepy little village, not armed or defended but a sanctuary for priests. They were no doubt surprised when none other than the famous David, the giant-killer, appeared in their village. This seemed unusual to Ahimelech the priest since David appeared to be traveling incognito without a royal entourage surrounding him. Ahimelech would have been curious to know why David had appeared in his doorway. Unfortunately, he was not going to get the truth.

Instead of telling Ahimelech the truth and trusting God to work through his honesty, David resorted to the means of natural men and lied. He told Ahimelech a tale that would eventually come back to bite him. He told the priest that he was on a secret mission from the king, the details of which he could not disclose. Instead of being an ambassador or envoy (as he pretended), David was a fugitive, running for his life.

David said one thing that was true—that he had left urgently. But he made it sound like the mission he was on for the king was so important that he was forced to leave quickly. In fact, he was forced to leave quickly because he was fleeing from the king. Nonetheless, as a result of leaving Saul's presence in a hurry, he had brought no provisions of food. So he asked Ahimelech for bread.

The only bread Ahimelech had available was the holy bread, or showbread, that had just been removed from before the Lord when fresh bread was put in its place. So he gave David several loaves of bread for him and his men. Ahimelech could be criticized for using this special bread inappropriately, just as David could be criticized for taking it. But in the mind of Jesus Christ, neither did wrong in appropriating the bread for David's needs. In Luke 6:1–5 Jesus used the story of David and the bread to point out that people and their needs are more important than religious ceremonies.

So neither Ahimelech nor David did wrong by using the showbread outside of its religious purpose. But that is not the main point of this story. What David did wrong was to lie to Ahimelech, to deceive another person in order to get what he wanted. He had no idea the amount of trouble he was creating for himself in doing this. Lying once normally sets in motion a string of lies—the necessity to tell more and more lies to cover the lies already told.

We need to note in passing the mention in 1 Samuel 21:7 of another man who was in the village of Nob that day: "Doeg, an Edomite, the chief of the herdsmen who *belonged* to Saul." Saul had eyes and ears in the village of Nob—something David had not known.

Then David told another lie: He had no sword with him because of leaving in such a hurry. It is hard to imagine a soldier, a policeman, a mighty warrior like David, leaving home without his weapon. As obvious as that seems to us, apparently Ahimelech didn't think it was out of order, so he offered David the only sword he had: the sword of Goliath the Philistine, captured by David when he killed the giant in the Valley of Elah.

So David took the oversized sword, strapped it to his waist, and left the village of Nob.

DAVID DEGRADED BEFORE ACHISH

First Samuel 21:10 says that David left Nob and fled to Gath, home of a king named Achish. If you recall from our study of Goliath, Gath was the region from which Goliath came—one of the areas where descendants of Anak (the giants) lived. How strange that David would pick Goliath's hometown as the place to seek sanctuary from Saul! Perhaps he thought people would have forgotten him by now, or that he could just walk in and get lost in the crowds and not be noticed. But such was not the case. The servants of Achish, the king, spotted him immediately—they even remembered the song that the women of Israel sang about Saul's thousands and David's ten thousands.

There's only one way they could have known David, since those who saw him were not likely on the battlefield that day: Goliath's sword. This sword was probably legendary in Gath—and was probably huge! If David had it strapped to his belt, it was likely dragging on the ground as he walked. It would have been just a little odd looking to say the least.

David's lie to Ahimelech resulted in David getting a sword that immediately identified who he was. He might as well have walked into Gath carrying a sign that said, "I killed Goliath." David realized his life was in danger and quickly came up with another scheme: He played like he was a madman. He started drooling all over his beard and banging on the gates of the city like he was crazy. Achish's response when David was brought before him was classic: "What do I need a madman for? Can't you see he's crazy? Get him out of here!" (1 Samuel 21:14–15, my paraphrase).

Remember: This is David, the anointed king of Israel, the man after God's own heart, acting this way. David lied to Ahimelech verbally and then lied to Achish nonverbally. His whole life in this series of events is a lie. It just goes to show how far a person is willing to go when they stop believing that God's way is best. David resorted to lies because he didn't think God was able to get him out of the situation he was in with Saul.

DAVID DELIVERED BEFORE ADULLAM

So David was kicked out of Gath (which was his goal in acting insane), and he fled to the cave of Adullam. Once word got out that David was in hiding in a cave, "everyone *who was* in distress, everyone who *was* in debt, and everyone *who was* discontented gathered to him. So he became captain over them. And there were about four hundred men with him." Can you imagine? By acting like part of the lunatic fringe, David attracted all the ne'er-do-wells, the riffraff, and the mercenaries in Judah to himself. But these men ultimately become his own private army, and they stick with him through battles yet to come.

The most important thing we will see in this lesson is what happened to David spiritually when he went into hiding in the cave of Adullam. Psalms 57 and 142 are two more examples of psalms that clearly reveal in the superscription when they were written: "A Michtam of David when he fled from Saul into the cave" (Psalm 57). From these psalms we get insight into what transpired spiritually at this time in David's life.

David was defiled before Ahimelech, degraded before Achish, and was now hiding in a cave, surrounded by hundreds of misfits. His own lying and scheming brought him to this point in his life. He was surrounded by people, yet he knew he was utterly alone before God. There was no one who could help him except God. He saw the cave he was in as a prison: "Bring my soul out of prison, that I may praise Your name" (Psalm 142:7). Finally, through these psalms, David did what he should have done much earlier: He called out to God for deliverance. But David was still in that place where he vacillated between belief and unbelief, and it showed up in his behavior.

At this time in David's life, we see what happens when we get out of fellowship with God and resort to the ways of the world to solve our problems. To a greater or lesser degree, this has happened to every Christian. I have made choices to try to solve problems my way instead of God's, and you probably have, too. We get determined to work things out ourselves and often have to fail miserably before we will admit we should have done things God's way.

APPLICATIONS

Here are the lessons I believe David probably learned from his choices, lessons we need to learn as well.

When You Are Out of Fellowship With God, You Seek Bad Counsel

At the end of 1 Samuel 19, David was in the presence of Samuel, the prophet of God. Remember, Samuel is the one who anointed David to be king, the one who heard from God. David had seen

Samuel work enough times to know that his counsel could be trusted. He should have confided in Samuel and asked for his help. Samuel knew the character of Saul; he knew Saul was trying to kill David. Samuel would have sought the Lord's counsel with David if David had just asked. Instead, David ended up with Jonathan, who was a good friend but was not a prophet.

If you want God's perspective on what you should do in your life, you need to ask godly people.

When You Are Out of Fellowship With God, You Select Bad Choices

It only follows that if you get bad advice, you are going to make bad choices. In David's case, no one told him to lie to Ahimelech and act insane at Gath. In a sense, he was getting counsel from himself. We make the mistake of thinking that because we are Christians, every thought we have is from God—that we don't need to seek His counsel on important matters. So we counsel ourselves, which is what David did. If he had stopped and cried out to the Lord in Jerusalem, he wouldn't have found himself crying out to the Lord in the cave of Adullam.

Recall the Edomite named Doeg we met in 1 Samuel 21:7. He was in Nob when David arrived looking for food and a sword; he witnessed Ahimelech aiding David. Once David and his men left the cave of Adullam, Doeg reported to Saul what Ahimelech had done. As a result, Saul told Doeg to kill Ahimelech and all the other priests in Nob—85 priests died. And Doeg killed every other living soul and all the livestock in the village.

I am sure David lived with that on his conscience for the rest of his life. Did God forgive him? Of course. But did God bring all those people back to life? No. Those were the unintended, indirect consequences of acting on his own without inquiring of the Lord.

We never know what is going to happen when we decide to act without first seeking the Lord and seeking godly counsel. I imagine David would take it all back if he could, but that is not how it works. What's done is done. Don't put yourself in that regrettable position. Seek the Lord for His guidance in everything you do.

1. When making significant decisions in your life, do you tend to seek counsel from others, or do you rely on your own judgment? Who do you most often turn to for guidance and why?

2. What is one of the characteristics of a wise person? (Proverbs 1:5)

3. How does Isaiah 28:29 commend God as the best of all possible counselors?

4. When confronted with the decision between truthfulness and dishonesty in both Nob and Gath, which did David choose? Did David's decisions reflect trust in the Lord?

5. What lies did David tell? Did anyone tell (counsel) David to lie? Why does one lie often set in motion a string of lies? What consequences did David face as a result of his lies?

6. What happened to David spiritually when he went into hiding in the cave of Adullam? What did he finally do that he should have done much earlier? (Psalm 57; 142)

7. Talk to God now about what you have learned in this lesson. If there are any decisions that need to be made in your own life, seek the Lord's guidance over these matters through prayer, for He is indeed your wonderful Counselor.

1. Discuss the following statement from the lesson: "Anyone is only a decision away from falling." Do you agree? Why or why not?

2. What can happen to people over time if there is no wise guidance? (Proverbs 11:14) Discuss examples of types of people (counselors) we can turn to for guidance. What is the practical advantage of a "multitude of counselors"? (Proverbs 24:6)

3. What significance do you find in the title "Counselor" appearing in Isaiah 9:6? To whom is this referring?

4. At this time in David's life, we see what happens when we resort to the ways of the world to solve our problems. What can we learn from David's experience?

   a. When we are out of fellowship with God, we seek _____ _____. Discuss the differences between bad counsel and godly counsel.

b. When we are out of fellowship with God, we select _____
   _____. What were the indirect consequences of
   David's decisions? What does this tell us about acting without
   first seeking the Lord and godly counsel?

5. Take time as a group to pray about this lesson and ask the Lord,
   our wonderful Counselor, for His direction over each of your lives.

DID YOU KNOW?

The bread that Ahimelech gave David to eat was the showbread,
also called the bread of the presence (Leviticus 24:5–9). This
latter name was used because it was placed on a golden table
in the presence of God in the holy place of the temple. The bread
consisted of twelve loaves placed in two rows of six loaves. It
functioned as a kind of grain offering to the Lord, and the loaves
were replaced with new ones each week. Ahimelech had loaves to
give David since he had just replaced the loaves with new ones.
Traditionally, the bread was to have been consumed by priests, but
Ahimelech took the liberty of meeting David's physical needs by
giving him the loaves.

A Prayer From a Cave

1 Samuel 22:1–2; Psalm 142

*In this lesson we learn how to move
from prison to praise.*

OUTLINE

The challenge in the Christian life is not learning how to avoid problems—trouble will find us in spite of our efforts to avoid it. The challenge is learning to move through the problems by staying focused on God. David started with problems but prayed his way through to praise.

   I. **David Verbalized the Situation Before God**

  II. **David Visualized the Situation Before God**

 III. **David Recognized Something About God**

 IV. **David Realized the Provision He Has in God**

  V. **David Arrived at the Place of Victory**

OVERVIEW

David is beloved as a biblical character for many reasons, not the least of which is his humanity. The Bible does not gloss over his sins or exalt his victories. David is who he is, and what you see is what you get. He is a man for all seasons who struggles to keep his behavior in line with his beliefs. And for that realism, all who read the Bible identify with him.

We last saw David at perhaps the lowest point in his life apart from his (yet to come) experience with Bathsheba. In his attempt to escape the murderous threats of Saul, David used lies and deceit while staying on the move. He ended up in a cave surrounded by hundreds of others attracted by his fugitive status. But none of these misfits could help David sort out the spiritual conflict in his soul. He was a man confused by what was happening to him and by his own actions. And he was a man with a guilty conscience after learning that a whole village and cadre of priests were wiped out as a result of his errant behavior.

At the beginning of 1 Samuel 22, we find David in the cave at Adullam with his brothers and parents and the hundreds who gathered with him. (We won't cover this in detail, but it is interesting to note that David sent his parents to Moab to gain the protection of Mizpah, the king. David was the great-grandson of Ruth, the Moabitess who married Boaz, and his family no doubt still had relatives and connections there. See 1 Samuel 22:3–4; Ruth 4:21–22; and Matthew 1:5.)

David's experience in the cave of Adullam is representative for many of us—a place of discouragement and confusion from which we cry out to the Lord. We have two psalms that are directly connected with this event, Psalms 57 and 142, and possibly part of a third, Psalm 34. There are eight psalms in Scripture that come from David's life as a fugitive, and these three are related to his experience in the cave.

The cave of Adullam was large—twenty feet wide and forty feet high at the opening, big enough to hold the large group of men that rallied around David at this time. Many of them were fugitives as well—many were in debt, possibly for failure to pay taxes Saul had levied upon the people. The crowd grew from 400 to 600 (1 Samuel 23:13) as word spread of David's presence at the cave. David found himself the leader of a huge contingent of distressed, indebted, and discontented men who made him their leader.

Of the two psalms, 57 and 142, I believe David probably wrote the latter first; so we will focus on Psalm 142 in this lesson. It is a short psalm of only seven verses and a psalm with which we can easily identify. All of us have been in our own caves at various times in life—the cave of financial trouble, family trouble, physical trouble. Whatever the trouble we have been in, we can identify with David in his cave experience.

And because David was a poet, a songwriter, he poured out the feelings of his heart in beautiful words. If I had been in David's place, I would have written, "Life is a cave in the pits"—and let it go at that. But David didn't write like that—his emotions were on his sleeve. We read and feel everything David was going through, which makes us appreciate his honesty and transparency.

In Psalm 142:3 David says his spirit was "overwhelmed" within him—in Hebrew, this Scripture literally means his spirit was "muffled." He felt like a flood had overwhelmed him, that his spiritual sensitivities were muffled by the affliction he was in. Today we might equate his feelings to trying to walk through a pool full of molasses—everything was in slow motion. He felt desensitized and disoriented. He probably felt like a businessman who returns from a two-week trip and finds his desk overflowing with papers and work awaiting his attention: "This is too much!" he might say. "I can't handle it!" He doesn't know where to start, so he doesn't. He just sits and stares at that which is confronting him.

Take that kind of disorientation and apply it on a much deeper level—the level of the soul. David had lost his friends; the king was his enemy; he had lied and acted deceitfully; he was indirectly responsible for the slaughter of an entire village and cohort of priests; his family was in danger; and he had become known as the leader of all the rabble in Judah. He's saying, "This is too much! I can't handle it! Where do I begin to sort out all of this mess?" It's easy to see why David felt like there was a giant woolen muffler wrapped around his senses.

Verse 4 is probably the saddest verse in the psalm: *"There is no one who acknowledges me; . . . no one cares for my soul."* Even though David was surrounded by hundreds of people, with more arriving daily, he still felt completely alone. He was saying, "These people can't possibly understand what I'm feeling, nor do they have any answers."

Once when my wife and I visited London, we were caught at rush hour in Piccadilly Circus (like the Times Square of London). We were told that there were probably a million people in our vicinity at that hour, all trying to get home. Donna and I tried to get on the train and almost got separated. We were packed in like sardines with a huge crowd of people we didn't know. It was a distinctly lonely feeling. Just because we're surrounded by people doesn't mean we are comforted by their presence.

We tend to think our problems are unique, that no one else has experienced what we are going through, so we withdraw. Who can we talk to? Who could possibly understand? There have been times in my life as a pastor, husband, and father that I wanted to talk with someone but wondered if anyone would really understand what I was feeling. Of course, our problems are not unique. Yes, the details may be different, but all of us go through the same feelings of loneliness, confusion, and despair at times. When we are in the midst of those feelings, we feel totally isolated.

I don't know if David was clinically depressed. But he was likely close to it. He had created a situation which he could see no way out of; he could see no light at the end of the tunnel. Many people today choose to end their life because they become so pessimistic about the possibility of finding solutions for their hopelessness. David may have been close to that point before he began to call upon the Lord. He had internalized all the trouble he was feeling, and it had become his identity. His problems were no longer objective, "out there." They were inside him, part of who he was.

Depression can be sin, or brought on by sin, but it is not necessarily sinful. Many spiritual people have struggled with severe discouragement or depression—Elijah, Jonah, Moses, David, and others. The great English preacher Charles Spurgeon would sometimes have to take a couple of months away from his preaching in order to pull himself out of his own dark night of the soul.

In verse 6 David says, "My persecutors . . . are stronger than I." That is a sign that he had created a mental ledger. On one side were all those who had something against him: Saul, Samuel, the relatives of the villagers of Nob, the family of Ahimelech, the king of Gath, the soldiers of Saul who were pursuing him. And on the other side of the ledger he put himself. If he weighed this out on a set of scales, it would be totally imbalanced. He would be completely outnumbered by those who had something against him. Tallying up both sides of the ledger produced this bottom line: David was in serious moral and spiritual debt and had no resources by which to balance the ledger. And what does the world do with debtors? They land in jail—which is how David viewed the cave of Adullam: "Bring my soul out of prison . . ." (verse 7). Sometimes our own caves feel like prisons, so we know how David felt. But it is also important to know that David worked his way through his feelings so that his last words in this psalm were, "For You shall deal bountifully with me." We need to see how he made the transformation from despair to belief so that we can follow his example in our own lives.

DAVID VERBALIZED THE SITUATION BEFORE GOD

Throughout this short psalm, David tells God how he feels: "I cry out to the LORD . . . I pour out my complaint . . . I cried out to You . . . Attend to my cry." You may ask, "Doesn't God already know how I feel?" Yes, He does. But the heart of communion is communication. We will tell our best friend how we feel, but we refuse to tell God. Why? Somehow we think God can't hear us or doesn't care or won't respond. But that is not the truth. The one Person in the universe with the resources to meet our needs is the very Person to whom we ought to be telling our needs. If you are in a cave of despair right now, you must begin by crying out to the Lord.

DAVID VISUALIZED THE SITUATION BEFORE GOD

In verse 2 we see David painting for God a verbal picture of the situation he is in: "I pour out my complaint before Him; I declare before Him my trouble." Eugene Peterson's *The Message* puts it like this: "I . . . spell out my troubles in detail."

A temptation for us when we pray is to rush into our supplication without spending time praising God. When we visualize our situation, we need to see it against a backdrop of God's greatness. And the way we visualize the greatness of God is by praising Him in prayer. When we put praise first in our prayers, we enlarge God in our hearts; we see Him for who He is, which puts our problems in proper perspective. If we put the problems ahead of the Solution, we run the risk of depressing ourselves even further.

David Recognized Something About God

In verse 3 David seems to get a glimpse of God's omniscience and omnipresence. Perhaps he hasn't been totally alone: "You knew my path." David is pouring out his heart to God and in that process realizes God has been watching over him the whole time. That is why we need to talk to God. In that process, we gain new insight and understanding. David could have been echoing the words of Job: "But He knows the way that I take; *when* He has tested me, I shall come forth as gold" (Job 23:10).

David Realized the Provision He Has in God

The more David prays and writes, the more he begins to realize that God is the one who can deliver him from the confusion he feels: "I said, 'You *are* my refuge, my portion in the land of the living'" (verse 5). The more he begins to praise God for who He is, the more it becomes clear to him that God will be able to see him through. A cave is not David's refuge—God is his refuge and his portion.

David Arrived at the Place of Victory

In the last verse, David arrives at the place of victory. He is no longer painting a verbal picture of the emotional and spiritual prison he is in. Instead, he asks God for what he needs: "Bring my soul out of prison, that I may praise Your name" (verse 7). David has gone from problems to praise! We find the same process going on in the other psalm David wrote from the cave, Psalm 57, where he also works his way from problems to praise. He goes from "My soul *is* among lions . . . whose teeth *are* spears and arrows" to "My heart is steadfast, O God, my heart is steadfast." And he concludes with a chorus we sing today, "Be exalted, O God, above the heavens; *let* Your glory *be* above all the earth."

You can make the same transformation in your life if you will follow David's pattern of prayer. You will find that your prison of problems becomes a palace of praise as you see God for who He is.

1. "All of us have been in our own caves at various times in life—the cave of financial trouble, family trouble, physical trouble. Have you ever found yourself in a cave of discouragement?" Describe your situation and how you felt at that time.

2. Why do you suppose we sometimes feel as though no one else could possibly understand the problems or trials we face?

3. Follow David's transformation from despair to belief by reading the verses from Psalm 142 below and then filling in the blanks.

   a. Verse 1: David _____ the situation before God.

   b. Verse 2: David _____ the situation before God.

   c. Verse 3: David _____ something about God.

   d. Verse 5: David _____ the provision he has in God.

   e. Verse 7: David _____ at the place of victory.

4. How comfortable are you with painting a verbal picture of your problems to God? Do you ever write out your own prayers— your own psalms? How do you think that might be helpful?

5. Why is it sometimes a temptation for us when we pray to rush into our supplication without spending time praising God? Is it your pattern in prayer to offer praise to God before your petitions? How do you think that would help?

1. Why is it that we can sometimes feel lonely or isolated, even when we are surrounded by other people?

2. How large was the cave of Adullam? How many people rallied around David at this time? (1 Samuel 23:13) Describe the types of people that surrounded David. In the midst of this crowd, how did David feel? (Psalm 142:4)

3. Is it sinful to feel depressed? What are some examples of other figures in the Bible who experienced severe discouragement or depression?

4. Read Psalm 142 aloud and discuss the questions below.

   a. In this psalm, David told God how he felt. Why is it important to tell the Lord how we feel?

   b. In verse 2, David painted a verbal picture for God of the situation he was in. How can we visualize the greatness of God? How can praising God put our problems in perspective?

c. What did David realize in verse 3? What does this tell us about the importance of talking to God?

d. In verse 5, we see David becoming encouraged as he realizes what truth?

e. What is the last step in David's transforming prayer? (verse 7)

5. As you close, share prayer requests and offer praise unto the Lord through prayer.

DID YOU KNOW?

Psalm 57 is one of a handful of psalms designated as a *miktam*. This term is found in the superscription of Psalms 16 and 56–60 and is always accompanied by "of David." Scholars are divided over the precise meaning of the term, thus English versions of the Bible do not translate the word, leaving it as *miktam* or *michtam*. All these psalms are of a similar length and style, making them able to be sung to the same tune: "Do Not Destroy" (Psalms 57–59). Psalm 16 has no tune designated, while Psalm 56 is set to the tune of "The Silent Dove in Distant Lands," and Psalm 60 is set to "Lily of the Testimony." Psalm 60 may contain a clue as to the purpose of a *miktam*: "For teaching."

HOW TO TREAT YOUR ENEMY

1 Samuel 24; Psalm 7

In this lesson we learn how to respond when attacked.

OUTLINE

At some point in life, everyone will be wronged or attacked by another. How do we respond? If we choose the way of the world, we can file a lawsuit or wage a retaliatory attack. But if we follow God's way, we seek to restore the relationship through reconciliation.

I. **Refuse Revenge**
    A. Refuse Revenge When Circumstances Seem to Allow for It
    B. Refuse Revenge When Counselors Stand to Advise It

II. **Risk Reconciliation**
    A. What David Risked
    B. What David Did

III. **Restore the Relationship**

R evenge and retaliation have become big business in our world. As I understand it, the United States is the most litigious country in the world with thousands of new lawsuits filed every day. Not all those lawsuits are motivated by revenge—but some of them are. With attorney fees running in the hundreds of dollars per hour, it costs thousands of dollars to take even a simple case to court. And there is even more revenge taken outside the courts—people acting against others to get back at them for something they did.

All of us have been wounded by another person at some time in our life, and all of us are tempted with the idea of seeking revenge. In this lesson we consider the possibility of David seeking revenge against Saul. A lawyer would have a field day with this case because David had done nothing to hurt Saul. For his own reasons of jealousy and anger, Saul began attacking David. From a purely human perspective, no one would blame David if he tried to pay Saul back for the pain he had inflicted on him.

To set the stage for this lesson, we learn in 1 Samuel 23 that Saul continued his attempts to capture David at various places but was not successful. At the end of the chapter we learn that a Philistine uprising had forced Saul to call off the hunt for David and return to deal with the Philistines. When that happened, David relocated to a place called En Gedi, near the Dead Sea.

We have discussed at length in previous lessons all that David had done himself—he made many mistakes and found himself in an unenviable position at the cave of Adullam. But we haven't focused as much on the injustices of Saul. David's behavior was without excuse, but the unrelenting pressure of Saul's attacks against David make it easier to understand. David had done nothing to deserve Saul's hatred. He had made Saul look good by defeating Goliath. He had won numerous battles against the Philistines by leading Saul's troops. He had brought relief to Saul when the evil spirit oppressed him. And for all that, Saul repaid him with jealousy and attempted murder. But still, David had attempted no retaliation.

Located twenty miles south of Jerusalem and about 600 to 900 feet above the Dead Sea plain, En Gedi was a stronghold of rough cliffs and mountains pockmarked by caves. First Samuel 24:2 refers to this place as the Rocks of the Wild Goats, a place fit only for cliff-climbing wild animals—and fugitives. After Saul dealt with the Philistines, he learned that David was holed up at En Gedi. He gathered a force of 3,000 soldiers and moved them into position to trap David.

David would soon be faced with the same question we are often faced with: What do we do when we have the opportunity to take revenge on someone who has wronged us?

REFUSE REVENGE

One option, of course, is to refuse revenge—the choice David made.

Refuse Revenge When Circumstances Seem to Allow for It

We rarely get the kind of detailed information that this story in 1 Samuel 24 provides, but it is crucial to our understanding. Saul went into a cave at En Gedi to relieve himself—the very cave in which David and his band of men were hiding. Suddenly, the odds were in David's favor! It had been 3,001 against 601—but suddenly it was 1 against 601. Saul had come into the cave alone, and David and his army of 600 were hiding silently in the recesses of the cave.

The circumstances certainly allowed for David to seek revenge against Saul. He could have snuck up behind him and taken the king's life. Out of the hundreds of caves at En Gedi that Saul could have gone into, he chose the one where David could easily have killed him.

Refuse Revenge When Counselors Stand to Advise It

When David and his men recognized who had come into the cave, David's men told him it was God's doing. God had brought David's enemy within striking distance in order for him to exact his revenge. Had they known Psalm 118:24, David's advisors might have quoted it to David: "This *is* the day the LORD has made; we will rejoice and be glad in it." Or Jeremiah 46:10: "For this *is* the day of the Lord GOD of hosts, a day of vengeance, that He may avenge Himself on His adversaries. The sword shall devour; it shall be satiated and made drunk with their blood. . . ."

David's advisors probably knew by now that David had been anointed as the next king. They wanted David to dispatch Saul so that David would take the throne and they would get plum assignments in the new administration. But here is another case where ungodly counsel, if taken, would be disastrous. David was being advised by ungodly men, receiving the kind of counsel God doesn't bless (Psalm 1:1).

Thankfully, David rejected the murderous counsel of his men. But he devised his own strategy which, while not totally honorable, at least had an honorable intent. He wanted to prove to Saul that he was still the king's loyal subject, so he crept up and cut a corner off Saul's robe while the king was tending to his business. He wanted to be able to prove to the king that he had been within striking distance but had stayed his hand. He wanted to demonstrate that he was not a vengeful person.

Not surprisingly, David's conscience bothered him afterward (1 Samuel 24:5). Even such a small act, cutting off a piece of the king's robe, was disrespectful; he was sorry he had done it (verse 6). David had maintained a sensitive heart toward God through all of this and knew the difference between complete honor and partial honor when it came to those in authority over him. By not harming Saul, David was taking to heart the principle that his own son, Solomon, would one day recount: "Do not say, 'I will do to him just as he has done to me; I will render to the man according to his work'" (Proverbs 24:29). We have to wonder if Solomon learned this principle from the story told to him by his father, David.

RISK RECONCILIATION

The reason more people don't attempt reconciliation is that it is risky. The primary risk is being rejected—being made to look like a fool. And that is a bigger risk than many people are willing to take.

What David Risked

There were two specific things David risked: ridicule and retaliation.

1. David Risked Ridicule

David risked being laughed at by his own men when he told them he felt bad about cutting a piece off Saul's robe—not to mention being ridiculed for not killing Saul outright. In fact, verse 7 says that he had to restrain his men to keep them from rising up against Saul.

Remember who David was talking to—600 of the most malcontent men in Israel. They would have thought nothing of taking the life of someone who deserved to die—maybe even someone who didn't. To put it in modern terms, they probably thought David was yellow. Here is the man who went out and killed a giant single-handedly, but he wouldn't kill the man who had caused him so much personal pain.

But David stood his ground and refused to stretch out his hand against the king. His strength and conviction were enough to bring his men to heel, and Saul left the cave unharmed.

Some people view reconciliation as weakness, but it isn't. It takes more strength to do what is right than to do what is wrong.

2. David Risked the Retaliation of Saul

Then David did an amazing thing. He went out of the cave and called out to Saul, revealing his hiding place. He bowed down before Saul to plead his case with the king.

What David Did

David presented the facts, proved his faithfulness, and pledged his friendship.

1. He Presented the Facts

Very simply, David stated his case to Saul: "The people you're listening to are giving you false reports. I'm not trying to harm you. I could have harmed you just now in the cave, but I didn't. Please believe that it is not my intent to harm the Lord's anointed."

Saul's advisors were apparently telling the king that David was seeking to harm him somehow. Obtaining secondhand information from people is a sure way to receive the wrong story. If you are in a conflict with someone, speak directly to him or her and present the facts in a clear, unemotional way, just as David did.

2. He Proved His Faithfulness

David actually proved that his words were true—he held up the corner of Saul's robe to show him that he could easily have killed him but didn't. Sometimes it takes an action on our part to demonstrate that our words are true: "Actions speak louder than words." The fact that David could have killed Saul but didn't lent support to David's words.

3. He Pledged His Friendship

Three times (verses 12, 13, and 15) David indicated his commitment to Saul. David pledged that he would not raise his hand against the king at all. In fact, David used what seemed to be a bit of humor with the king in verse 14. It is as if he were saying, "Saul, look what you're doing. You're the king of Israel with 3,000 men out here in the wilderness pursuing a dead dog—a flea! What are you thinking?" David tried to get Saul to see how unreasonable his actions were and how much more reasonable it would be for them to remain friends.

RESTORE THE RELATIONSHIP

After refusing revenge and risking reconciliation, the third principle for how to treat your enemy is to restore the relationship if at all possible. It appears that David's efforts have not been in vain. In 1 Samuel 24:16–21 Saul professed that he would drop his pursuit of David.

Saul was confronted with such an outright demonstration of grace and humility from David that he was overcome with emotion and began to weep. These weren't the tears of repentance or conversion. Rather, they were the tears of pent-up emotion. For months Saul had been consumed with hatred for David. His actions were in such stark contrast to David's humility that all the emotion came pouring out.

Saul realized he was standing face-to-face with the man who would replace him on the throne and that his successor was the better man. In fact, he said, "You *are* more righteous than I" (verse 17). We have to wonder if Saul recalled the words of Samuel to him when he disobeyed the Lord in the incident with the Amalekites. At that point, Samuel told Saul that the kingdom was being given to his neighbor "*who is* better than you" (1 Samuel 15:28). Saul met the better man at En Gedi.

Then Saul asked David to do something that would cement the restored relationship and benefit Saul's descendants after he was gone. Saul was hardly in a place to ask for a favor from David, but he did. Instead of asking for David's forgiveness, he was still centered only on himself. He asked David to swear that he would not exercise vengeance upon any of his descendants, that his name would not be cut off and forgotten in Israel. (David kept this promise by restoring the grandson of Saul, Mephibosheth, to the royal household after both Saul and Jonathan were dead— 2 Samuel 9.) David, in a generous gesture, swore an oath to Saul to protect his descendants.

Did Saul change as a result of David's generous spirit toward him? No. Unfortunately, forgiving someone doesn't mean they are going to change. Do we still have a responsibility to forgive? Yes, we do. Think of David's situation: He had no guarantee that Saul would indeed leave him alone. In fact, he probably knew Saul wouldn't. But he wasn't responsible for Saul; he was only responsible for his own actions and attitudes: "Right now, regardless of the past or the future, I forgive you. I can't control what you may do or think, but I can control what I do and think. And I choose to release my animosity toward you and forgive you in the same way God has forgiven me." David refused to exact vengeance, risked reconciliation, and restored the relationship.

Many believe Psalm 7 was written in connection with David's experience with Saul. The key words in that psalm are in verses 10 and 11: "My defense *is* of God, who saves the upright in heart. God *is* a just judge." David decided to let God be God as far as Saul was concerned and do what he knew was right for him to do. If you will choose to do the right thing by seeking to restore relationships, God will be your defense just as He was David's.

PERSONAL QUESTIONS

1. Think of a time when you were wounded by another person. How did you respond? Were you tempted with the idea of revenge?

2. What had David done to deserve Saul's hatred?

3. In 1 Samuel 24:1–4, what opportunity arose?

   a. What did David's men advise him to do?

   b. Who did they believe had orchestrated these circumstances? (verse 4)

   c. Did David heed their counsel?

   d. From this example, what can we learn about receiving counsel from others?

4. What did David do instead? (1 Samuel 24:4b) What was his motivation for doing this? How did he feel about his decision afterward? Why? (verse 5)

5. Why is attempting reconciliation risky? What three steps did David take to reconcile with Saul? Fill in the blanks.

   a. He presented the _____.

   b. He proved his _____.

   c. He pledged his _____.

6. Was David's attempt at reconciliation successful? What did Saul ask of David? How did David respond to Saul's request? (1 Samuel 24:16–21)

7. Did Saul change as a result of David's generous spirit toward him? Does forgiving someone mean they are going to change? Do we still have a responsibility to forgive?

8. What have you learned in this lesson that you can apply to a relationship in which you have been wronged?

GROUP QUESTIONS

1. Which response to conflict do we see most often in our culture today: reconciliation or revenge?

2. Why does modern society sometimes view reconciliation as the "weak" response? Do you think it takes more strength to reconcile with a person or to exact revenge?

3. When David went out of the cave and called out to Saul, revealing his hiding place, what great risk was he taking?

4. How did David's attempt at reconciliation demonstrate that "actions speak louder than words"? Was David successful in restoring his relationship with Saul? (1 Samuel 24:16–21)

5. Read Romans 12:17–21.

   a. What is Paul's clear command to Christians in verse 17?

   b. What should be our personal goal in all our relationships?

   c. On whom does Paul put the responsibility for living in peace? (verse 18)

   d. What is the best way to overcome evil? (verse 21)

6. What encouragement can we find in Psalm 7:10–11?

7. As you close in prayer, allow time for the members of the group to pray silently. If there are any relationships in which you have been wronged, or in which you have wronged another, ask the Lord to be your help as you seek to restore the relationship.

DID YOU KNOW?

E n Gedi, where David and his men hid from Saul, became prominent, supporting a village in biblical times, for one reason: fresh water. Not far from the shores of the Dead Sea, En Gedi was in the midst of dry, brackish wilderness. But a free-flowing spring of fresh water broke the surface about 600 feet above the Dead Sea—and in that region, a source of fresh water attracted people and settlements. Because of the fresh water, En Gedi became known for its vineyards and date palms. Archaeologists have discovered ruins at En Gedi dating back to the seventh century B.C.

DAVID AND ABIGAIL

1 Samuel 25

*In this lesson we learn the value
of heeding wise counsel.*

OUTLINE

It is typical of many in the Christian life to go from the mountain peak of victory to the valley of defeat. That happened to David when he reconciled with Saul at En Gedi and then planned to murder someone who offended him. The intervention of a godly woman saved him.

I. **The Foolish Farmer**

II. **The Furious Soldier**

III. **The Faithful Wife**
    A. Abigail Was Good
    B. Abigail Was Gracious
    C. Abigail Was Gallant
    D. Abigail Was Godly

D avid's encounter with Saul at En Gedi allowed for a temporary truce between the two men, a truce aided by another event in Israel: the death of Samuel. When Samuel died, it caused a national period of mourning in Israel out of respect for the man of God who had been at the center of Israel's life for so long. Undoubtedly, Saul decided it would be inappropriate to continue to take up arms against David during this time of mourning.

In light of the truce, David decided to put some distance between him and Saul and headed for the Wilderness of Paran, south of Judah. Because Paran was near the border, it was subject to raids by neighboring Philistines and Amalekites who would attack shepherds and landowners in the region. As a defense against these attacks, small armies of mercenaries like David's band would provide protection for shepherds and farmers and be compensated for their services.

Thus our story picks up in 1 Samuel 25 with David requesting support from a wealthy landowner named Nabal, whose shepherds had received protection from David's men while they were in the field (verses 15–16). This was the understood arrangement: In return for protection, owners of land and livestock would provide food and other necessities for those who protected them.

Apparently in need of supplies, David sent ten of his men to Nabal—a rich but evil man (verses 2–3). David's men approached Nabal at the time of the year when he was shearing his sheep. This was like the harvest time of the year when a great deal of money exchanged hands between buyers and sellers. David knew Nabal would have resources to share, so he sent his men to request payment for the services they had provided to Nabal's shepherds. There was no demand for a specific amount to be paid, just a request for help. David probably wasn't expecting money as much as he hoped to get food stores for his men.

The story that developed is a tale of three people: a foolish farmer, a furious soldier, and a faithful wife.

THE FOOLISH FARMER

Nabal is characterized in several ways in this story, first as a very wealthy man. He lived in the region of Paran, but his livestock business was in Carmel, farther to the north in Israel. He had large holdings in sheep (3,000) and goats (1,000) and was shearing the sheep in Carmel. This was a time of great festivity—eating and drinking and merrymaking in celebration of a successful year of business.

Connected to Nabal's wealth was another characteristic—his wickedness. Based on his response to David's men when they approached him, his wickedness probably was a manifestation of his greed. He apparently became wealthy not by being generous but by being stingy. He was "harsh and evil in *his* doings," verse 3 says, meaning he was obnoxious and overbearing and rude and unreasonable—not a person one would enjoy being around. He was wealthy and wicked, rich and rude, prosperous and pompous all at the same time. One of the men who worked for Nabal referred to him as a "scoundrel" (in the Hebrew, "son of Belial," or "son of the devil"), impossible to reason with (verse 17).

If you really want to know what a man is like, ask his wife. When Nabal's wife, Abigail, talks with David about Nabal later in the story, she describes him as Nabal's employee did: a scoundrel, a fool (verse 25). The word *nabal* in Hebrew is the word for "fool," and there apparently has never been anyone more aptly named than Nabal. As Abigail said to David, "Nabal *is* his name, and folly *is* with him!" Today we think of a fool as being like a court jester in the Middle Ages—a comedian or silly person. Not so in the Old Testament. In that world a fool was a moral failure, a man who lived independent of God and His wisdom, a man who failed to learn from the error of his ways and correct them, a man who had no moral compass to guide him through life.

Nabal was a man who thought that because of his wealth and position, he could receive protection from David and his men and ignore their services. He had no sense of fair play at all. He pretended he did not know who David was, suggesting he might be just some rebellious mercenary trying to extort money from wealthy people like himself. It would have been impossible to live in Israel at that time and not know who David was!

Nabal definitely lived up to his name, and he would soon reap what he sowed.

THE FURIOUS SOLDIER

When David received the report from the ten men he sent to Nabal, he had one reply: "Every man gird on his sword" (1 Samuel 25:13). It was David's intent to go to Carmel and kill Nabal and every one of his male heirs—effectively wipe his name off the face of the earth (verses 22, 34).

David was furious over being rebuffed by Nabal; in a fashion typical of all of us at times, he overreacted. To deal with one man, David took 400 of his own men—sort of the equivalent of Saul coming after David with 3,000 soldiers. But that is how angry he was at the words of the morally-deficient Nabal. All the way from Paran to Carmel, David was seething (verses 21–22). I imagine his thoughts were like this: "I have had enough! There is no excuse for this sorry sheepherder to treat me like this. I have done everything a man could do to help him, and then he throws it in my face. If I let this go by, I won't be able to look myself in the mirror. No one can mess with me like this! I might have to take this kind of stuff from the anointed of the Lord, but I am not going to be treated like this by a common farmer. He's dead meat!"

To say the least, David was furious with Nabal, the foolish farmer.

THE FAITHFUL WIFE

As is often the case, God sent an incredibly wise woman to check the spirit and intent of a furious man. Abigail has to be one of the unsung heroines of the Old Testament. Her wisdom and understanding in how to handle a volatile situation were just remarkable. We can find a number of commendable qualities of Abigail throughout the story.

Abigail Was Good

Most noticeable is the stark contrast between Nabal and Abigail. He was amoral, but she was a good woman, an upright person, "a woman of good understanding" (1 Samuel 25:3). But not only was she morally sound, a wise woman, she was beautiful as well.

Abigail Was Gracious

Besides wisdom and beauty, she was also characterized by grace. Six times in her conversations with David, she described herself as a maidservant; eight times she referred to David as "lord" (meaning "master"), actually bowing down before him. Laced throughout the dialogue we find her saying "please" to David. In other words, Abigail knew her place in this situation. She was no fan of her husband, but she also knew that David was a wise and honorable man. Though he had a right to be angry, Abigail knew how to appeal to David and humble herself before him to keep him from doing something foolish.

Abigail was the opposite of Nabal, which shows that it is possible to live with someone who is a fool without becoming foolish yourself. She maintained her character, not sinking to the depths at which her husband Nabal lived.

Abigail Was Gallant

Besides being good and gracious, Abigail was also gallant. When one of Nabal's servants learned that David was on his way to kill Nabal, he didn't warn Nabal—he went to Abigail. (The servants knew who to turn to when wisdom was needed.) He explained what David had done to protect the shepherds when they were in the field, and Abigail immediately sprang into action. She loaded up a mule train with an incredible abundance of food from Nabal's stores and headed out to intercept David.

Abigail had no way of knowing how David might respond, so her actions were courageous to say the least. But she took the initiative to stop a needless slaughter. Yes, Nabal deserved David's wrath. But slaughtering him and his sons was needless in order for David to make his point, and she was willing to stand in the way.

Abigail Was Godly

Finally, Abigail was godly, as revealed in three distinct ways:

First, Abigail knew David had been faithful to God (verse 28). She had heard of David's exploits (more evidence that Nabal had also heard of David) in defeating Goliath and the Philistines and how he had faithfully protected the shepherds.

Second, she knew God had been faithful to David (verse 29). Perhaps she knew that Saul had pursued David all around Judah and yet had been unable to lay a hand on him: "Yet a man has risen to pursue you and seek your life. . . ." But she declared that David would be protected and his enemies slung out "*as from* the pocket of a sling." This woman had incredible discernment—she knew who God was protecting and blessing. She even spoke prophetically about David's future, saying the Lord would make for him an "enduring house" (verse 28).

Third, Abigail knew that sin was tenacious (verses 30–31). She knew that David was destined to become the king of Israel. She appealed to him not to let a petty grievance with Nabal mar his character and reputation. It wasn't worth whatever satisfaction he would receive from killing Nabal to have a guilty conscience as the king of Israel. Better to become king with clean hands than with hands covered with the blood of a man who was not worth killing.

Abigail knew that sin doesn't go away; it would continually haunt David all his days.

David was duly impressed with Abigail's counsel. He took her advice, accepted the gift of food she brought, and cancelled his plans. It is a wise man who listens to the counsel of a wise woman.

When Abigail returned home, she found Nabal feasting as part of the shearing celebration. Because he was full of wine, she waited until morning to talk with him. The next morning when Abigail told Nabal what she had done, something very strange happened: "[Nabal's] heart died within him, and he became *like* a stone." Scholars believe this is a description of what we would today call a stroke. The shock of what Abigail had done caused Nabal to react so violently (internally) that he had a stroke. And within ten days he was dead (verses 37–38).

By withholding vengeance, David was blessed by God, and his enemy was eliminated by natural causes. It is another example of how the Lord will fight our battles for us if we will only let Him.

David had two responses to Nabal's death. The first was to praise the Lord for doing in His own way what would have been terrible if David had done it (verse 39). And the second was much more important to David: He recognized the depth of character and wisdom of Abigail and invited her to be his wife. David was no fool! He recognized immediately what a powerful woman Abigail was and knew he would be better off with her by his side. When Abigail received David's proposal for marriage, she did not hesitate to accept. She knew David was the kind of man with which she wanted to be.

There are three characters in this story, and a word of application can be drawn from each:

There are many Nabals in the world and probably some in the Church as well—people who think they can flaunt God's standards and get away with it, people who think they can live their life independent of God and not reap the consequences.

There are also many Abigails, people who are determined not to be influenced by the environment in which they live, people who are determined to follow God's ways of wisdom regardless of what others do.

And then there are Davids, people who can experience victory one day (like David did at En Gedi) and be tempted to murder someone the next!

The spiritual life is a daily contest between the flesh and the Spirit. We learn from Nabal that we will reap what we foolishly sow. We learn from Abigail that there are rewards for wisdom. And we learn from David how to submit to wise counsel and not get carried away by prior spiritual victories. May God grant wisdom as we learn lessons from each one.

PERSONAL QUESTIONS

1. What type of person do you visualize when you envision a foolish person? What type of person did the word "fool" refer to in the Old Testament?

2. What characteristics described Nabal? How was Nabal described by his employee? By his wife?

3. When David sent his men to request payment for the services they had provided to Nabal's shepherds, how did Nabal respond? When David received word of this, what was his reaction? (1 Samuel 25:13, 21–22)

4. How did Abigail's character compare to her husband's character? List the four descriptions of Abigail from this lesson:

   a. Abigail was _____.

   b. Abigail was _____.

   c. Abigail was _____.

   d. Abigail was _____.

5. When Abigail received word that David was on his way to kill Nabal, what did she do? What wise counsel did she give to David? Did David heed her words?

6. The next morning, when Abigail reported what she had done to Nabal, what happened?

7. How did David respond to Nabal's death?

8. With which character from this story do you identify most: Nabal, David, or Abigail? Why? What lessons can you draw from each person's conduct in this chapter?

GROUP QUESTIONS

1. Based on this story from Scripture, describe what a Nabal in today's world might look like. In other words, what type of person would he/she be? What might an Abigail in today's society look like? A David?

2. How does Psalm 49:10 describe what happened to Nabal?

3. Read the correlating verses from Proverbs concerning "fools" to answer the questions below.

   a. Proverbs 12:15: What does a fool think of his opinions?

   b. Proverbs 14:16: Contrast the way wise and foolish men react to the presence of evil.

c. Proverbs 15:7: What can a wise person do that a fool cannot?

d. Proverbs 17:28: In what instance is a fool actually considered insightful?

e. Proverbs 20:3: Why is there more honor in ending a quarrel than in starting one?

f. Proverbs 29:11: How does self-control keep a person from being a fool?

4. Discuss the life lessons we can take away from each of the characters we examined in this chapter: the foolish farmer, the furious soldier, and the faithful wife.

5. As we read in this lesson, "The spiritual life is a daily contest between the flesh and the Spirit." As you close in prayer, ask the Lord to grant you the wisdom needed to be victorious each day.

DID YOU KNOW?

At the end of the episode with Nabal, we have information about David's wives. Michal, the first wife and daughter of Saul, had been given to another man (1 Samuel 25:44). David took for his wife two others: Abigail, the widow of Nabal from Carmel, and Ahinoam of Jezreel. In 2 Samuel 3:2–5 we have a list of the wives David had during his seven-year reign at Hebron once he was king. Besides Abigail and Ahinoam, there was Maacah, the daughter of the king of Geshur; Haggith (background unknown), Abital (background unknown), and Eglah (background unknown). Political alliances were often cemented by marriages (for example, Solomon's marriage to the daughter of the pharaoh to seal a treaty with Egypt—1 Kings 3:1).

DAVID'S DEEP DEPRESSION

1 Samuel 27; 30

*In this lesson we discover the dangers of
discouragement and depression.*

OUTLINE

It can begin simply—a failed expectation, a disappointing moment,
a success not achieved. If we don't keep every event in its proper
perspective and stay focused on the Lord, disappointment can lead
to depression. From David's experience, we see where that can lead.

I. **The Circumstances of David's Depression**
    A. He Had an Enemy He Could Not Master
    B. He Had an Expectation He Could Not Meet

II. **The Cost of David's Defection**
    A. He Deceived Himself
    B. He Dishonored God
    C. He Destroyed His Testimony
    D. He Descended Into Further Sin

Depression and discouragement are common in the human experience. Even if one is never diagnosed as clinically depressed, requiring psychiatric treatment, almost everyone has occasional times when life takes on a dull shade of gray, when it sounds like we're wearing winter earmuffs over our ears, when food loses its flavor and nature her colors.

Discouragement is no respecter of persons. Even great men of God like Charles Haddon Spurgeon have suffered its effects. Spurgeon wrote of his own experience,

> Before any great achievement, some measure of . . .
> depression is very usual. . . . Such was my experience when
> I first became a pastor in London. My success appalled
> me. . . . Who was I that I should continue to lead so great a
> multitude? . . . It was just then that the curtain was rising
> upon my life-work . . . . This depression comes over me
> whenever the Lord is preparing a larger blessing for
> my ministry.[1]

It is true that whenever the Lord is preparing a larger blessing for any ministry, depression often accompanies it.

The curtain was definitely rising on David's ministry. Yet in 1 Samuel 27, we find him wallowing in self-inflicted misery and depression. The psalms David wrote during this period are truly dark, giving evidence of a man looking up from the bottom of a deep pit of despair. They are the words of a great hero that become easier to understand as we study this period of David's life.

THE CIRCUMSTANCES OF DAVID'S DEPRESSION

We are introduced to David's depression immediately in the first verse of 1 Samuel 27:

> Now I shall perish someday by the hand of Saul. *There is*
> nothing better for me than that I should speedily escape
> to the land of the Philistines; and Saul will despair of me,
> to seek me anymore in any part of Israel. So I shall escape
> out of his hand.

There were two reasons David was depressed: He had an enemy he couldn't master and an expectation he couldn't meet.

He Had an Enemy He Could Not Master

We passed over chapter 26 because of its similarity to the experience at En Gedi where David cut off a piece of Saul's robe to show that he could have killed the king but spared his life. This time, Saul and his troops were again in pursuit of David (in spite of the truce Saul agreed to at En Gedi), and David again had the opportunity to take his life. Instead, he snuck into Saul's camp and took Saul's spear and water jug from beside the sleeping king. He then stood on a nearby mountain and called out to Saul, and an exchange ensued similar to the one at En Gedi: Saul expressed remorse and promised to stop pursuing David. As David knew at En Gedi, he knew that Saul's words were hollow this second time as well. He knew that Saul would be his pursuer as long as both of them were alive.

Every day, David lived with the knowledge that Saul was after him. The pressure was relentless—there was never a day off. It was probably the last thing David thought about at night and the first thing he thought about in the morning. Even when Saul was miles away, he might as well have been right next to David—so perpetual was his presence in David's thoughts. Saul was an enemy David could not master.

We occasionally have those kinds of enemies in our life as well. It may be a disease or a financial obligation, unemployment, or a wayward child that has left home. It is an enemy we live with daily. Whenever our minds take a break from an immediate task at hand, that enemy appears in our thoughts. And in time, with that enemy comes another: discouragement, despair, even depression.

There is even another enemy we have, a spiritual one, who is just as relentless. Saul is a perfect picture of Satan, the lion who prowls about seeking whom he might destroy (1 Peter 5:8). Though we have spiritual defenses to use against Satan, the fact that we can never let those defenses down is a picture of how David felt with Saul. David wasn't so much worried about losing his life to Saul as he was tired from the daily pressure of having to be on his guard. Such is our weariness that comes from living on our spiritual guard as well.

He Had an Expectation He Could Not Meet

David had several thousand people who were dependent upon him for their provision: his army of 600, plus their wives and children. Moving these people from place to place in Judah got to be such a burden that he crossed the border into Philistia and threw himself on the mercy of Achish, the king.

David himself had two wives at this point in his life (1 Samuel 25:42–44; 27:3) and I'm sure felt a particular burden to care for the wives and children of his soldiers. It was one thing to lead a group of men, but quite another to lead a group that included many hundreds of wives and children. David basically said, "I can't do this anymore. If I leave Judah and go into Philistine territory, perhaps we can escape the pressure of Saul's relentless pursuit." He settled in Gath, the home village of Goliath, whom he had killed, and the plan worked. Saul dropped his pursuit temporarily when he learned that David was with the Philistines (1 Samuel 27:4). David settled among his pagan enemies and soon began to act like them.

Life can get that way for us. We throw up our hands and say, "I can't keep up with all that I'm responsible for and do it in a spiritual way. I'm going to move over into the world, where nothing will be expected of me until I can catch my breath." Too often, abandoning our spiritual priorities while we take a break turns into a long-term lifestyle decision that we come to regret. When the pressures become too great, it is easy to lose our perspective and our focus and start living like the world.

The question is not whether those pressures will come in life— they most certainly will. The question is, "What do we do about them when they come?" Notice in 1 Samuel 27:1 what "David said in his heart. . . ." There was no prayer or counsel involved. David just took it upon himself to make this decision. Impulse mixed with passion and panic can lead to bad decisions.

THE COST OF DAVID'S DEFECTION

The rest of this chapter details the consequences of David's decision to move in among his pagan neighbors. David was depressed, and then he defected—and he paid a dear price.

He Deceived Himself

To see how David deceived himself, recall why Saul wanted him out of Judah. It was so David could not ascend to the throne. David accomplished for Saul exactly what Saul wanted to happen! David thought he was getting Saul off his back, which he did. But he also made it impossible to become the next king of Israel. How could a king of Israel come from among the Philistines?

David was deceived into thinking he was safe from Saul, and he was. But that did not mean he was safe. He was living in the midst of people who were much more dangerous than Saul had ever been. He jumped out of the proverbial frying pan and into the fire when he moved from Judah to Gath. He was now in the homeland of Goliath, the homeland of the people who had been a thorn in Israel's side for years. And he apparently did not see it.

To put it mildly, there are some cures worse than the disease. When you and I adopt the ways of the world as a strategy for dealing with our problems, we put ourselves in much greater peril than we were before.

He Dishonored God

It is important to remember that God had clearly communicated to David that he was to be the next king of Israel—Samuel, God's prophet, had anointed David with oil and spoken God's words concerning his future. Jonathan, Saul's son and David's best friend —the one who stood to lose the most from David's ascension to the throne—also declared that David would be the next king and gave David his royal robe as a sign (1 Samuel 18:4). And then Abigail, David's wife, confirmed the same thing, that David was destined to rule over Israel (1 Samuel 25:30). Even Saul, David's enemy, knew and said that David was to replace him as king (1 Samuel 24:20).

But listen to David's own words: "Now I shall perish someday by the hand of Saul" (1 Samuel 27:1). He didn't say, "I'm going to be king." He said, "I'm going to die. I'll never be king." David totally dishonored God by saying the exact opposite of what God said.

If we could see a printed record of our own thoughts the way we can see David's, we might see that we are just as contradictory at times. Look at David's words in Psalm 27:1: "The LORD *is* my light and my salvation; whom shall I fear? The LORD *is* the strength of my life; of whom shall I be afraid?" Now contrast that with, "Now I shall perish someday by the hand of Saul." What happened to David? Where was his faith?

The same thing that happened to David can happen to us if we allow discouragement and deception to replace sound spiritual judgment.

He Destroyed His Testimony

Philistia was a rank, pagan culture. There was no way for David to continue to grow spiritually in the long run by leaving

God's culture and moving into a pagan culture. Judah wasn't perfect, but it was a more spiritual place than Philistia, where idol worship was the order of the day.

Achish, the king of Gath, gave David and his people the city of Ziklag as a place to dwell. So David and his men and their families moved to the southern region of Philistia to Ziklag, a city originally included in the allocation of land for the tribe of Judah (Joshua 15:21–31). Ziklag was eventually captured by the Philistines and was lost to Judah. Ironically, the future king of Judah moved in and made Ziklag his home base of operations.

There were Jews, those who had originally settled the city, living in Ziklag but who were now under the control of the enemy, the Philistines who had captured the city. And now David moved in to join those who were living in a compromising position in terms of their faith. It is a picture of how the people of God, even Christians today, can belong to God but be controlled and dominated by Satan. It is a quick way to ruin one's testimony—to say, "I belong to God" but to live under the control of the enemy. It is one thing to find yourself surrounded by the enemy when it is beyond your control, but it is another thing to choose to live among the enemy.

He Descended Into Further Sin

It is difficult to deceive oneself, dishonor God, and destroy your testimony without descending further into sin.

The only means David had of supporting his army and their families was to plunder from others. So he began invading neighboring nations and stealing their cattle and goods and killing the inhabitants. The nations he raided were peoples that had a history of attacking Israel, so at least David was preying on the enemies of God—at least he didn't cross into Israel and steal and plunder from his own people. But that was the only good thing about what he was doing. What he did was a form of genocide: He literally wiped villages off the map, leaving nothing of value and no one breathing. He left no one alive so word couldn't get back to King Achish of Gath as to what David was doing. David was telling Achish that he was actually raiding Judah! To Achish, this meant David would never be able to return home, and he would be David's ally forever.

David was living in a world of murder, lies, and deception. It is incredible where his discouragement and despair led him!

David's big mistake was in verse 1 of chapter 27: "David said in his heart. . . ." We should never make big life decisions when discouraged or despairing. David finally got things turned around when his own soldiers began to rebel against him: "But David strengthened himself in the LORD his God" (1 Samuel 30:6). This time, instead of talking and listening to himself, he began to talk and listen to God.

Here's how to strengthen yourself in the Lord:

1. Focus on promises.

2. Focus on prayer.

3. Focus on the possibilities.

No matter how dark the day and how discouraging the developments, it is possible to get refocused on God. When we do that, He will meet us where we are and shed new light on our path —a path that leads us from darkness to life.

Note

1. Charles H. Spurgeon, *Lectures to My Students*, Volume 1.

PERSONAL QUESTIONS

1. Reflect on a time when you felt depressed or deeply discouraged. What were the circumstances?

2. Review the circumstances of David's depression. He had an
_____ he could not master and an
_____ he could not meet.

3. Read 1 Peter 5:8.

   a. Who is your enemy?

   b. In what way is Saul a perfect picture of this enemy?

4. Compare David's words in Psalm 27:1 to his words in 1 Samuel 27:1.

a. What differences do you see in his attitude?

b. How were his words in 1 Samuel 27:1 dishonoring to God? What other big mistake did David make in this verse? (Hint: "David said in his heart. . . .")

5. David finally got things turned around when he "strengthened himself in the LORD his God" (1 Samuel 30:6). According to the lesson, in times of discouragement, what three steps can you take to strengthen yourself in the Lord?

   a. Focus on _____.

   b. Focus on _____.

   c. Focus on _____.

6. Take time to select several promises from Scripture that you can hold onto during trying times and write them down below. Consider challenging yourself to commit these verses to memory so you are prepared when you need them most.

GROUP QUESTIONS

1. How can feelings of discouragement and despair affect the way we make decisions?

2. What impulsive decision did David make that cost him dearly?

3. Why did Saul want David out of Judah? In what way did David accomplish for Saul exactly what Saul wanted? Did fleeing to Gath ensure David's safety? What can we learn from this example?

4. Read 1 Samuel 27:1 aloud.

   a. How were David's words contradictory to what God had said?

b. What can happen to us when we allow discouragement and deception to replace sound spiritual judgment?

5. What type of culture was Philistia? How could David have profited from the advice in 1 Corinthians 15:33 when he fled to Gath with his army? What are Christians in danger of if they are not careful?

6. How did David support his army and their families? What did David tell Achish, the king of Gath? What can we learn from David's downward spiral into sin?

7. How did David finally get things turned around? (1 Samuel 30:6) What does it mean to strengthen yourself in the Lord?

8. As you close, pray for strength to remain focused upon the Lord through every circumstance of life.

DID YOU KNOW?

The painful words of David in Psalm 22:1 were echoed by Christ on the cross (Matthew 27:46). Concerning such heartfelt prayers, John Calvin wrote,

The true rule of praying is, therefore, this, that he who seems to have beaten the air to no purpose, or to have lost his labor in praying for a long time, should not, on that account, leave off, or desist from that duty. Meanwhile, there is this advantage which God in his fatherly kindness grants to his people, that if they have been disappointed at any time of their desires and expectations, they may make known to God their perplexities and distresses, and unburden them, as it were, into his bosom. (*Calvin's Commentary* on Psalm 22)

TWO MEN IN MISERY

1 Samuel 28–29

In this lesson we examine the devastating results of sin.

OUTLINE

It has been said that sin can outbreed a rabbit. That's because one sin almost always leads to another. The deeper we get mired in sin, the harder it is to extract ourselves from it. The safest way to avoid such trouble is to avoid sin—or repent of it immediately when it happens.

I.   The Misery of David

II. The Misery of Saul
   A. The Fear of Saul
   B. The Failure of Saul
   C. The Fall of Saul

III. The Moral of Their Stories
   A. The Plurality of Sin
   B. The Potential of Sin
   C. The Power of Sin

To understand a developing story, especially a mystery, you have to start at the beginning and follow all the threads that are running parallel. That is what we have been doing with the story of Saul and David. Eventually, Saul will drop out of the picture—we are near that point now. But so far in this study guide, we have studied both of their lives because they are so intertwined. Eventually, when we get to the end of the story, we see how all the pieces fit together.

We left David in our last lesson having abandoned his homeland and, in a state of depression, moving to the neighboring pagan Philistine region of Gath. There he became part of a godless culture. He became like the Philistines he used to fight against—a ruthless warrior who obliterated entire villages and all their inhabitants, plundering their property to support his own soldiers and their families.

David got to this terrible place by getting counsel from himself instead of God (1 Samuel 27:1). He was willing to go around God's standards whenever it suited him—lying and deceit seemed to be his besetting sins. It is no wonder he wrote in Psalm 119:29, "Remove from me the way of lying, and grant me Your law graciously." When we lie to others, we also lie to God (Psalm 51:4) and to ourselves. David had deceived himself into thinking that he was ultimately going to die at the hands of Saul—that God's promises to him wouldn't stand—and so took matters into his own hands.

We never know where our path will lead when we allow ourselves to be deceived. For David the path was a downward one that led to dark places.

THE MISERY OF DAVID

David continued to live under the rule of the Philistine king, Achish, lying to him about his activities. To curry favor with Achish and convince him of his loyalty, David had been telling him that he had been attacking and plundering Judean cities. So Achish considered David a loyal subordinate and member of his royal retinue: "Therefore I [Achish] will make you [David] one of my chief guardians forever" (1 Samuel 28:2).

David went to Gath to hide from Saul—a seemingly simple, low-profile objective. Then, a year later, he found himself the bodyguard of the king! David, the future king of Israel, had gotten himself situated at the right hand of the king of the Philistines. What a sad state of affairs for a man who was supposed to be seeking after the heart of God.

The Philistines were gathering to make war against Israel, and he was expected to participate. If he said "No," he would be in trouble with Achish; if he said "Yes," he would eventually be reviled in Israel, branded for life as a traitor. He was in a mess—exactly where lies and deceit always led. When you seek help from the world, there will always be a price to pay.

THE MISERY OF SAUL

Our story switches now to Saul—he gathered his armies to defend Israel against the invading Philistines but was scared to death (1 Samuel 28:3–5). Samuel was dead and Saul had no one to tell him what was going to happen. He inquired of the Lord but, not surprisingly, the Lord did not answer him (verse 6).

The Fear of Saul

Saul had been cut off from God for so long that fear was his basic response to threatening situations. He was one of those people who only called on God when trouble hit, only to discover that God wasn't talking back.

Saul had a guilty conscience. He had disobeyed Samuel, murdered Ahimelech and the other priests at Nob (along with the residents of the village), hunted David like an animal, lied to David about ceasing his persecution of him—the man was a walking defiled conscience. Now with the Philistines gathering on the horizon, he was shaking in his sandals with fear. Nothing is worse than being out of the will of God and staring a crisis in the face.

I have had people tell me that, because of their ungodly lifestyle, they were so consumed with fear that they took out extra life insurance in case God struck them dead. Being out of the will of God, and knowing it, is a fearful thing.

The Failure of Saul

"The LORD did not answer" are some of the saddest words in the Bible (verse 6). Saul had waited until it was too late to reestablish a relationship with God, and he was trying only because the enemy was knocking at the door. Had he been sincere, he would have first taken time to confess and repent of his sins. Isaiah the prophet would write many years later, "Seek the LORD while He may be found, call upon Him while He is near" (Isaiah 55:6). Saul failed to do that and was now unable to hear from God at all.

It is a mistake to think that God will stand for being ignored and then come running like a bellhop when we call on Him. I cannot say what God will or won't do, but I would not advise doing what Saul did: to ignore God and disobey Him and then expect Him to answer when we call. Psalm 66:18 explains why: "If I regard iniquity in my heart, the Lord will not hear." I have actually heard people say that they planned to do things they knew were not in God's will and then ask for forgiveness afterward. Such prayers will not be answered unless there is genuine confession and repentance of sin.

The Fall of Saul

The final nail in Saul's coffin is found in 1 Samuel 28:7 where, in lieu of hearing from God, he decided to consult a medium—a fortuneteller—to try to get some guidance from beyond the grave.

Verse 3 records the fact that Saul had previously "put the mediums and spiritists out of the land." That act was to his credit, but now he goes looking for a medium to consult for himself. And we are told in 1 Chronicles 10:13 that this is one of the primary reasons God judged Saul and took his life. Saul was trying to live with one foot in the right and one in the wrong. But in spiritual matters, that is impossible, not to mention hypocritical. Jesus said we cannot serve God and the world at the same time (Matthew 6:24). (It is worth noting that David was trying to do the same thing—fighting against the Philistines last year, fighting with them this year.)

Saul's servants found a medium, a woman in En Dor, for Saul to consult. Saul was there to engage in necromancy—communicating with the dead. He disguised himself and went in to the woman and asked her to call up Samuel from the grave so he could inquire of Samuel about the coming war with the Philistines. When she made contact with Samuel, he told Saul that he and his sons would be killed and the army of Israel would be defeated by the Philistines.

We need to stop and clarify the experience Saul had with the medium at En Dor. First, it should never have happened—consulting mediums and spiritists was well-known in Israel to be a violation of God's commands (Deuteronomy 18:9–11). Isaiah asked the most pertinent question about this practice: "*Should they seek* the dead on behalf of the living?" (Isaiah 8:19)

There are three explanations that have been offered as to how this happened—how Samuel appeared to give (what appears to be credible) information about the future to Saul.

First, some suggest that the medium concocted the whole thing, that nothing really happened.

Second, others suggest the witch caused a semblance of Samuel to appear, but that it wasn't really Samuel speaking the truth.

Third—and this is what I believe happened—it was the Lord who spoke to Saul. There is a basis for this view in Ezekiel 14:3, 7–8. Because Israel had set up idols in the land, from which people were seeking guidance, God issued a decree through Ezekiel that He would answer them Himself—and then cut them off from His people. If this is what happened in Saul's case, then it was God Himself who intervened and told Saul through Samuel what he wanted to know—and then, as we will see, cut him off. Anyone who tries today to get a glimpse into the future by consulting a medium or attending a séance ought to be ready for a similar outcome.

When the king of Israel visited a medium, that was the last straw. Saul and his sons would be dead in a matter of days.

THE MORAL OF THEIR STORIES

When we catch up with David at the beginning of chapter 29, we find that the princes of the Philistines were not happy about him going to war with them against Israel—they were afraid he would be a turncoat, that he would side with Israel and attack the Philistines. God used this fact to remove David from the sticky situation he had become involved in. Achish yielded to the pressure from his princes and sent David back home to Ziklag. God came to his aid once again. David pretended to be upset with Achish, but inside he was counting his blessings.

Both Saul and David were in miserable situations. Saul's downward spiral continued until he hit bottom, but David was delivered by God yet again. It is important to remember that God didn't deliver David because he was acting righteously but because God had promised David that he would become king. God was giving David a chance to work through the flaws in his character in preparation for assuming the throne of Israel.

In the midst of Saul's and David's misery, three lessons come to the surface.

The Plurality of Sin

It is almost impossible for a person to commit just one sin. The theologian Francis Schaeffer once wrote that whenever we break one of the Ten Commandments, we break two—because we also break the commandment not to covet whenever we break one of the others. Someone once said, "A single sin can outbreed an Australian rabbit." Sin breeds sin. Telling one lie usually involves telling more in order to keep the trail of the first lie covered. David found himself so entrapped by his own deviousness that he almost ended up going to war against his own people. The best way to avoid such entrapment is by not committing the first sin. That which doesn't exist can't multiply.

The Potential of Sin

When we step back and look at the situation we are studying in this lesson, it is almost hard to believe. We are studying two of the kings of God's chosen people, Saul and David. And in studying them, we're dealing with lies, deceit, killing and pillaging, necromancy, jealousy, rage, envy, attempted murder, consulting mediums, and more lies. If you say, "How could this have happened?" then you don't understand the potential for sin that exists in the heart of every human.

The old saying is true: The best of us are capable of the worst, and the worst of us are capable of the best. When we met David, we thought he was surely the best; yet he was involved in the worst—and the same with Saul. (Saul's namesake, on the other hand, Saul of Tarsus [the apostle Paul], was among the worst who became among the best.) Don't ever think that you are too good to sin or too lofty to fall. Many are the proud who have fallen.

The Power of Sin

James 1:15 says, "Then, when desire has conceived, it gives birth to sin; and sin, when it is full-grown, brings forth death." Sin has tremendous power—it can bring forth death in all those who consume it. Sin is what killed Saul (1 Chronicles 10:13–14), "For the wages of sin *is* death. . . ." (Romans 6:23).

We have to explain why sin killed Saul but not David. Why was David spared and Saul taken? The first factor to consider is God's sovereignty. God had chosen David to be king over Israel, and that meant he was going to become king. But we only know that in hindsight. We should never presume upon God's sovereignty as an excuse to commit our own sins.

Second to consider is the fact that David had a heart for God, something clearly stated in Scripture (1 Samuel 13:14; Acts 13:22). Somewhere beneath David's immaturity and his conniving ways beat a heart that wanted to know God and do His will.

God forgives repentant sinners—He always has. The question for us is not whether we have sinned, but whether we are people after God's own heart who want to do His will. If we are, God will forgive us and sustain us just as He did David.

1. What does it mean to be a faithful person? An unfaithful person?

2. Read 1 Chronicles 10:13–14.

   a. What is the first word in verse 13 that summarizes why Saul died?

   b. What are the two primary reasons God took Saul's life? (verse 13b)

3. Between the listing of Saul's sins and the statement that God "killed him" is this phrase: "But [Saul] did not inquire of the LORD." What does this mean? Might Saul's future have been different if he had taken these sins to the Lord?

4. Once Saul died, what happened to the kingdom? (verse 14)

5. Why was David's life spared and Saul's taken? (Romans 6:23; 1 Samuel 13:14; Acts 13:22)

6. In your own words, explain the three principles you learned about sin from this lesson.

7. Read Isaiah 55:6–7.

   a. What should the wicked and the unrighteous do? (verse 7a)

b. What will God do when the unrighteous turn to Him? (verse 7b)

c. What does verse 6 imply about the availability of that mercy and pardon?

d. Is there any sin that you have delayed confessing to God? If so, what risk are you running?

1. Read Psalm 66:18 aloud. Discuss the meaning of this Scripture as a group.

2. When Saul saw the army of the invading Philistines, what was his response? What happened when Saul inquired of the Lord? (1 Samuel 28:3–6) What had Saul failed to do?

3. Discuss the following statement from the lesson: "Sin breeds sin."

   a. What does this mean?

   b. Have you found this principle to be true in your own life?

4. Speculate how things might have been different if Saul, immediately following the judgment of 1 Samuel 15:23, had stepped down from the throne and turned the kingdom over to David. How might both of their lives have been different? What lessons do you see demonstrated in that scenario?

5. What comfort does 1 John 1:9 give every believer about God's mercy toward those who are repentant of their sin?

6. How does 1 Corinthians 10:11–12 apply to anyone who has read about the stories of Saul and David?

7. If time allows, share what you learned from part one of this study that most deeply resonated with you. What did you learn that you perhaps did not know before beginning this study? Was there anything you were surprised to learn?

God was unequivocal about His prohibition on the practices of the pagan nations Israel would encounter when they entered the Promised Land:

When you come into the land which the LORD your God is giving you, you shall not learn to follow the abominations of those nations. There shall not be found among you *anyone* who makes his son or his daughter pass through the fire, *or one* who practices witchcraft, *or* a soothsayer, or one who interprets omens, or a sorcerer, or one who conjures spells, or a medium, or a spiritist, or one who calls up the dead. (Deuteronomy 18:9–11)

It was in part because of a violation of these laws that Israel was taken into exile (2 Kings 17:17).

SLAYING THE GIANTS

Whether you are battling fear, anger, temptation, jealousy, loneliness, resentment, worry, or discouragement, this series will motivate you to stand up to the daunting foes you face. In this giant-slaying manual, Dr. David Jeremiah will help you claim eternal promises that will enable you to slay the spiritual giants in your life and live victoriously.

COURAGE TO CONQUER

In the *Courage to Conquer* series, we meet some of the Bible's greatest heroes: Paul, Joshua, David, Habakkuk, Isaiah, and three Hebrew men who faced a notorious king. History is full of heroes, but these few chose freedom over safety and did not give in to the threats of those who sought to take away that freedom. In this series, Dr. David Jeremiah teaches us how, with God's guidance, we too can live with the courage to conquer.

MY HEART'S DESIRE

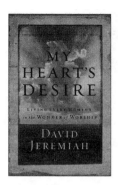

The wonder of worship has been lost in the lives of many today. But God's desire for us is that we live in constant worship every day, making it a moment-by-moment reality in our lives. In *My Heart's Desire,* Dr. David Jeremiah teaches us how to experience the wonder and amazement of the presence of God by maintaining a daily lifestyle of worship.

OVERCOMING LONELINESS

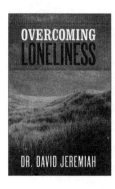

Loneliness may well be the prevailing disease of our time. No one, married or single, religious or nonreligious, young or old, is exempt from the pain. Though we are all susceptible to loneliness at some point in our lives, we can overcome it and fill that aching void. In *Overcoming Loneliness,* Dr. Jeremiah points out several positive methods for healing this disease of the soul. This resource will not only help you find encouragement for your own heart but will help you to know how to help others overcome the bondage of loneliness.

Each of these resources was created from a teaching series by Dr. David Jeremiah. For more information about correlating materials contact Turning Point.

For pricing information and ordering, contact us at

P.O. Box 3838
San Diego, CA 92163
(800) 947-1993
WWW.DAVIDJEREMIAH.ORG